Mometrix
TEST PREPARATION

I0889381

CISA®

Exam Secrets Study Guide

DEAR FUTURE EXAM SUCCESS STORY

First of all, **THANK YOU** for purchasing Mometrix study materials!

Second, congratulations! You are one of the few determined test-takers who are committed to doing whatever it takes to excel on your exam. **You have come to the right place.** We developed these study materials with one goal in mind: to deliver you the information you need in a format that's concise and easy to use.

In addition to optimizing your guide for the content of the test, we've outlined our recommended steps for breaking down the preparation process into small, attainable goals so you can make sure you stay on track.

We've also analyzed the entire test-taking process, identifying the most common pitfalls and showing how you can overcome them and be ready for any curveball the test throws you.

Standardized testing is one of the biggest obstacles on your road to success, which only increases the importance of doing well in the high-pressure, high-stakes environment of test day. Your results on this test could have a significant impact on your future, and this guide provides the information and practical advice to help you achieve your full potential on test day.

Your success is our success

We would love to hear from you! If you would like to share the story of your exam success or if you have any questions or comments in regard to our products, please contact us at **800-673-8175** or **support@mometrix.com**.

Thanks again for your business and we wish you continued success!

Sincerely,
The Mometrix Test Preparation Team

Need more help? Check out our flashcards at:
http://MometrixFlashcards.com/CISA

Written and edited by the Mometrix Exam Secrets Test Prep Team
Printed in the United States of America

TABLE OF CONTENTS

Introduction

Thank you for purchasing this resource! You have made the choice to prepare yourself for a test that could have a huge impact on your future, and this guide is designed to help you be fully ready for test day. Obviously, it's important to have a solid understanding of the test material, but you also need to be prepared for the unique environment and stressors of the test, so that you can perform to the best of your abilities.

For this purpose, the first section that appears in this guide is the **Secret Keys**. We've devoted countless hours to meticulously researching what works and what doesn't, and we've boiled down our findings to the five most impactful steps you can take to improve your performance on the test. We start at the beginning with study planning and move through the preparation process, all the way to the testing strategies that will help you get the most out of what you know when you're finally sitting in front of the test.

We recommend that you start preparing for your test as far in advance as possible. However, if you've bought this guide as a last-minute study resource and only have a few days before your test, we recommend that you skip over the first two Secret Keys since they address a long-term study plan.

If you struggle with **test anxiety**, we strongly encourage you to check out our recommendations for how you can overcome it. Test anxiety is a formidable foe, but it can be beaten, and we want to make sure you have the tools you need to defeat it.

Secret Key 1: Plan Big, Study Small

There's a lot riding on your performance. If you want to ace this test, you're going to need to keep your skills sharp and the material fresh in your mind. You need a plan that lets you review everything you need to know while still fitting in your schedule. We'll break this strategy down into three categories.

Information Organization

Start with the information you already have: the official test outline. From this, you can make a complete list of all the concepts you need to cover before the test. Organize these concepts into groups that can be studied together, and create a list of any related vocabulary you need to learn so you can brush up on any difficult terms. You'll want to keep this vocabulary list handy once you actually start studying since you may need to add to it along the way.

Time Management

Once you have your set of study concepts, decide how to spread them out over the time you have left before the test. Break your study plan into small, clear goals so you have a manageable task for each day and know exactly what you're doing. Then just focus on one small step at a time. When you manage your time this way, you don't need to spend hours at a time studying. Studying a small block of content for a short period each day helps you retain information better and avoid stressing over how much you have left to do. You can relax knowing that you have a plan to cover everything in time. In order for this strategy to be effective though, you have to start studying early and stick to your schedule. Avoid the exhaustion and futility that comes from last-minute cramming!

Study Environment

The environment you study in has a big impact on your learning. Studying in a coffee shop, while probably more enjoyable, is not likely to be as fruitful as studying in a quiet room. It's important to keep distractions to a minimum. You're only planning to study for a short block of time, so make the most of it. Don't pause to check your phone or get up to find a snack. It's also important to **avoid multitasking**. Research has consistently shown that multitasking will make your studying dramatically less effective. Your study area should also be comfortable and well-lit so you don't have the distraction of straining your eyes or sitting on an uncomfortable chair.

The time of day you study is also important. You want to be rested and alert. Don't wait until just before bedtime. Study when you'll be most likely to comprehend and remember. Even better, if you know what time of day your test will be, set that time aside for study. That way your brain will be used to working on that subject at that specific time and you'll have a better chance of recalling information.

Finally, it can be helpful to team up with others who are studying for the same test. Your actual studying should be done in as isolated an environment as possible, but the work of organizing the information and setting up the study plan can be divided up. In between study sessions, you can discuss with your teammates the concepts that you're all studying and quiz each other on the details. Just be sure that your teammates are as serious about the test as you are. If you find that your study time is being replaced with social time, you might need to find a new team.

Secret Key 2: Make Your Studying Count

You're devoting a lot of time and effort to preparing for this test, so you want to be absolutely certain it will pay off. This means doing more than just reading the content and hoping you can remember it on test day. It's important to make every minute of study count. There are two main areas you can focus on to make your studying count.

Retention

It doesn't matter how much time you study if you can't remember the material. You need to make sure you are retaining the concepts. To check your retention of the information you're learning, try recalling it at later times with minimal prompting. Try carrying around flashcards and glance at one or two from time to time or ask a friend who's also studying for the test to quiz you.

To enhance your retention, look for ways to put the information into practice so that you can apply it rather than simply recalling it. If you're using the information in practical ways, it will be much easier to remember. Similarly, it helps to solidify a concept in your mind if you're not only reading it to yourself but also explaining it to someone else. Ask a friend to let you teach them about a concept you're a little shaky on (or speak aloud to an imaginary audience if necessary). As you try to summarize, define, give examples, and answer your friend's questions, you'll understand the concepts better and they will stay with you longer. Finally, step back for a big picture view and ask yourself how each piece of information fits with the whole subject. When you link the different concepts together and see them working together as a whole, it's easier to remember the individual components.

Finally, practice showing your work on any multi-step problems, even if you're just studying. Writing out each step you take to solve a problem will help solidify the process in your mind, and you'll be more likely to remember it during the test.

Modality

Modality simply refers to the means or method by which you study. Choosing a study modality that fits your own individual learning style is crucial. No two people learn best in exactly the same way, so it's important to know your strengths and use them to your advantage.

For example, if you learn best by visualization, focus on visualizing a concept in your mind and draw an image or a diagram. Try color-coding your notes, illustrating them, or creating symbols that will trigger your mind to recall a learned concept. If you learn best by hearing or discussing information, find a study partner who learns the same way or read aloud to yourself. Think about how to put the information in your own words. Imagine that you are giving a lecture on the topic and record yourself so you can listen to it later.

For any learning style, flashcards can be helpful. Organize the information so you can take advantage of spare moments to review. Underline key words or phrases. Use different colors for different categories. Mnemonic devices (such as creating a short list in which every item starts with the same letter) can also help with retention. Find what works best for you and use it to store the information in your mind most effectively and easily.

Secret Key 3: Practice the Right Way

Your success on test day depends not only on how many hours you put into preparing, but also on whether you prepared the right way. It's good to check along the way to see if your studying is paying off. One of the most effective ways to do this is by taking practice tests to evaluate your progress. Practice tests are useful because they show exactly where you need to improve. Every time you take a practice test, pay special attention to these three groups of questions:

- The questions you got wrong
- The questions you had to guess on, even if you guessed right
- The questions you found difficult or slow to work through

This will show you exactly what your weak areas are, and where you need to devote more study time. Ask yourself why each of these questions gave you trouble. Was it because you didn't understand the material? Was it because you didn't remember the vocabulary? Do you need more repetitions on this type of question to build speed and confidence? Dig into those questions and figure out how you can strengthen your weak areas as you go back to review the material.

Additionally, many practice tests have a section explaining the answer choices. It can be tempting to read the explanation and think that you now have a good understanding of the concept. However, an explanation likely only covers part of the question's broader context. Even if the explanation makes perfect sense, **go back and investigate** every concept related to the question until you're positive you have a thorough understanding.

As you go along, keep in mind that the practice test is just that: practice. Memorizing these questions and answers will not be very helpful on the actual test because it is unlikely to have any of the same exact questions. If you only know the right answers to the sample questions, you won't be prepared for the real thing. **Study the concepts** until you understand them fully, and then you'll be able to answer any question that shows up on the test.

It's important to wait on the practice tests until you're ready. If you take a test on your first day of study, you may be overwhelmed by the amount of material covered and how much you need to learn. Work up to it gradually.

On test day, you'll need to be prepared for answering questions, managing your time, and using the test-taking strategies you've learned. It's a lot to balance, like a mental marathon that will have a big impact on your future. Like training for a marathon, you'll need to start slowly and work your way up. When test day arrives, you'll be ready.

Start with the strategies you've read in the first two Secret Keys—plan your course and study in the way that works best for you. If you have time, consider using multiple study resources to get different approaches to the same concepts. It can be helpful to see difficult concepts from more than one angle. Then find a good source for practice tests. Many times, the test website will suggest potential study resources or provide sample tests.

Practice Test Strategy

If you're able to find at least three practice tests, we recommend this strategy:

Untimed and Open-Book Practice

Take the first test with no time constraints and with your notes and study guide handy. Take your time and focus on applying the strategies you've learned.

Timed and Open-Book Practice

Take the second practice test open-book as well, but set a timer and practice pacing yourself to finish in time.

Timed and Closed-Book Practice

Take any other practice tests as if it were test day. Set a timer and put away your study materials. Sit at a table or desk in a quiet room, imagine yourself at the testing center, and answer questions as quickly and accurately as possible.

Keep repeating timed and closed-book tests on a regular basis until you run out of practice tests or it's time for the actual test. Your mind will be ready for the schedule and stress of test day, and you'll be able to focus on recalling the material you've learned.

Secret Key 4: Pace Yourself

Once you're fully prepared for the material on the test, your biggest challenge on test day will be managing your time. Just knowing that the clock is ticking can make you panic even if you have plenty of time left. Work on pacing yourself so you can build confidence against the time constraints of the exam. Pacing is a difficult skill to master, especially in a high-pressure environment, so **practice is vital**.

Set time expectations for your pace based on how much time is available. For example, if a section has 60 questions and the time limit is 30 minutes, you know you have to average 30 seconds or less per question in order to answer them all. Although 30 seconds is the hard limit, set 25 seconds per question as your goal, so you reserve extra time to spend on harder questions. When you budget extra time for the harder questions, you no longer have any reason to stress when those questions take longer to answer.

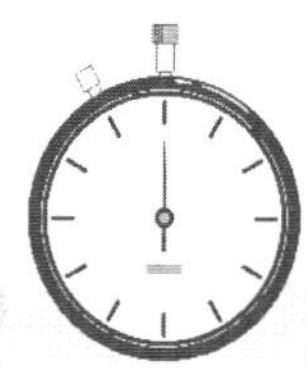

Don't let this time expectation distract you from working through the test at a calm, steady pace, but keep it in mind so you don't spend too much time on any one question. Recognize that taking extra time on one question you don't understand may keep you from answering two that you do understand later in the test. If your time limit for a question is up and you're still not sure of the answer, mark it and move on, and come back to it later if the time and the test format allow. If the testing format doesn't allow you to return to earlier questions, just make an educated guess; then put it out of your mind and move on.

On the easier questions, be careful not to rush. It may seem wise to hurry through them so you have more time for the challenging ones, but it's not worth missing one if you know the concept and just didn't take the time to read the question fully. Work efficiently but make sure you understand the question and have looked at all of the answer choices, since more than one may seem right at first.

Even if you're paying attention to the time, you may find yourself a little behind at some point. You should speed up to get back on track, but do so wisely. Don't panic; just take a few seconds less on each question until you're caught up. Don't guess without thinking, but do look through the answer choices and eliminate any you know are wrong. If you can get down to two choices, it is often worthwhile to guess from those. Once you've chosen an answer, move on and don't dwell on any that you skipped or had to hurry through. If a question was taking too long, chances are it was one of the harder ones, so you weren't as likely to get it right anyway.

On the other hand, if you find yourself getting ahead of schedule, it may be beneficial to slow down a little. The more quickly you work, the more likely you are to make a careless mistake that will affect your score. You've budgeted time for each question, so don't be afraid to spend that time. Practice an efficient but careful pace to get the most out of the time you have.

Secret Key 5: Have a Plan for Guessing

When you're taking the test, you may find yourself stuck on a question. Some of the answer choices seem better than others, but you don't see the one answer choice that is obviously correct. What do you do?

The scenario described above is very common, yet most test takers have not effectively prepared for it. Developing and practicing a plan for guessing may be one of the single most effective uses of your time as you get ready for the exam.

In developing your plan for guessing, there are three questions to address:

- When should you start the guessing process?
- How should you narrow down the choices?
- Which answer should you choose?

When to Start the Guessing Process

Unless your plan for guessing is to select C every time (which, despite its merits, is not what we recommend), you need to leave yourself enough time to apply your answer elimination strategies. Since you have a limited amount of time for each question, that means that if you're going to give yourself the best shot at guessing correctly, you have to decide quickly whether or not you will guess.

Of course, the best-case scenario is that you don't have to guess at all, so first, see if you can answer the question based on your knowledge of the subject and basic reasoning skills. Focus on the key words in the question and try to jog your memory of related topics. Give yourself a chance to bring the knowledge to mind, but once you realize that you don't have (or you can't access) the knowledge you need to answer the question, it's time to start the guessing process.

It's almost always better to start the guessing process too early than too late. It only takes a few seconds to remember something and answer the question from knowledge. Carefully eliminating wrong answer choices takes longer. Plus, going through the process of eliminating answer choices can actually help jog your memory.

Summary: Start the guessing process as soon as you decide that you can't answer the question based on your knowledge.

How to Narrow Down the Choices

The next chapter in this book (**Test-Taking Strategies**) includes a wide range of strategies for how to approach questions and how to look for answer choices to eliminate. You will definitely want to read those carefully, practice them, and figure out which ones work best for you. Here though, we're going to address a mindset rather than a particular strategy.

Your odds of guessing an answer correctly depend on how many options you are choosing from.

Number of options left	5	4	3	2	1
Odds of guessing correctly	20%	25%	33%	50%	100%

You can see from this chart just how valuable it is to be able to eliminate incorrect answers and make an educated guess, but there are two things that many test takers do that cause them to miss out on the benefits of guessing:

- Accidentally eliminating the correct answer
- Selecting an answer based on an impression

We'll look at the first one here, and the second one in the next section.

To avoid accidentally eliminating the correct answer, we recommend a thought exercise called **the $5 challenge**. In this challenge, you only eliminate an answer choice from contention if you are willing to bet $5 on it being wrong. Why $5? Five dollars is a small but not insignificant amount of money. It's an amount you could afford to lose but wouldn't want to throw away. And while losing $5 once might not hurt too much, doing it twenty times will set you back $100. In the same way, each small decision you make—eliminating a choice here, guessing on a question there—won't by itself impact your score very much, but when you put them all together, they can make a big difference. By holding each answer choice elimination decision to a higher standard, you can reduce the risk of accidentally eliminating the correct answer.

The $5 challenge can also be applied in a positive sense: If you are willing to bet $5 that an answer choice *is* correct, go ahead and mark it as correct.

Summary: Only eliminate an answer choice if you are willing to bet $5 that it is wrong.

Which Answer to Choose

You're taking the test. You've run into a hard question and decided you'll have to guess. You've eliminated all the answer choices you're willing to bet $5 on. Now you have to pick an answer. Why do we even need to talk about this? Why can't you just pick whichever one you feel like when the time comes?

The answer to these questions is that if you don't come into the test with a plan, you'll rely on your impression to select an answer choice, and if you do that, you risk falling into a trap. The test writers know that everyone who takes their test will be guessing on some of the questions, so they intentionally write wrong answer choices to seem plausible. You still have to pick an answer though, and if the wrong answer choices are designed to look right, how can you ever be sure that you're not falling for their trap? The best solution we've found to this dilemma is to take the decision out of your hands entirely. Here is the process we recommend:

Once you've eliminated any choices that you are confident (willing to bet $5) are wrong, select the first remaining choice as your answer.

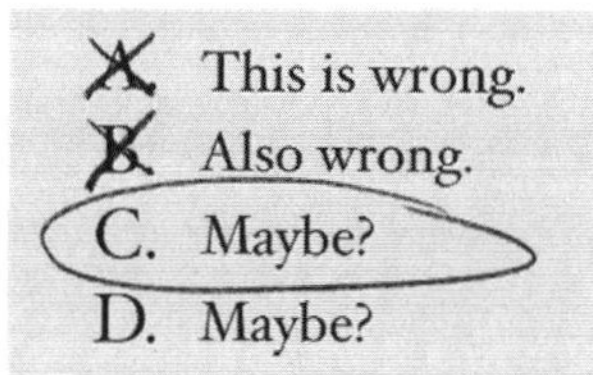

Whether you choose to select the first remaining choice, the second, or the last, the important thing is that you use some preselected standard. Using this approach guarantees that you will not be enticed into selecting an answer choice that looks right, because you are not basing your decision on how the answer choices look.

This is not meant to make you question your knowledge. Instead, it is to help you recognize the difference between your knowledge and your impressions. There's a huge difference between thinking an answer is right because of what you know, and thinking an answer is right because it looks or sounds like it should be right.

Summary: To ensure that your selection is appropriately random, make a predetermined selection from among all answer choices you have not eliminated.

Test-Taking Strategies

This section contains a list of test-taking strategies that you may find helpful as you work through the test. By taking what you know and applying logical thought, you can maximize your chances of answering any question correctly!

It is very important to realize that every question is different and every person is different: no single strategy will work on every question, and no single strategy will work for every person. That's why we've included all of them here, so you can try them out and determine which ones work best for different types of questions and which ones work best for you.

Question Strategies

✅ Read Carefully

Read the question and the answer choices carefully. Don't miss the question because you misread the terms. You have plenty of time to read each question thoroughly and make sure you understand what is being asked. Yet a happy medium must be attained, so don't waste too much time. You must read carefully and efficiently.

✅ Contextual Clues

Look for contextual clues. If the question includes a word you are not familiar with, look at the immediate context for some indication of what the word might mean. Contextual clues can often give you all the information you need to decipher the meaning of an unfamiliar word. Even if you can't determine the meaning, you may be able to narrow down the possibilities enough to make a solid guess at the answer to the question.

✅ Prefixes

If you're having trouble with a word in the question or answer choices, try dissecting it. Take advantage of every clue that the word might include. Prefixes can be a huge help. Usually, they allow you to determine a basic meaning. *Pre-* means before, *post-* means after, *pro-* is positive, *de-* is negative. From prefixes, you can get an idea of the general meaning of the word and try to put it into context.

✅ Hedge Words

Watch out for critical hedge words, such as *likely, may, can, often, almost, mostly, usually, generally, rarely,* and *sometimes.* Question writers insert these hedge phrases to cover every possibility. Often an answer choice will be wrong simply because it leaves no room for exception. Be on guard for answer choices that have definitive words such as *exactly* and *always.*

✓ Switchback Words

Stay alert for *switchbacks*. These are the words and phrases frequently used to alert you to shifts in thought. The most common switchback words are *but*, *although*, and *however*. Others include *nevertheless, on the other hand, even though, while, in spite of, despite*, and *regardless of*. Switchback words are important to catch because they can change the direction of the question or an answer choice.

✓ Face Value

When in doubt, use common sense. Accept the situation in the problem at face value. Don't read too much into it. These problems will not require you to make wild assumptions. If you have to go beyond creativity and warp time or space in order to have an answer choice fit the question, then you should move on and consider the other answer choices. These are normal problems rooted in reality. The applicable relationship or explanation may not be readily apparent, but it is there for you to figure out. Use your common sense to interpret anything that isn't clear.

Answer Choice Strategies

✓ Answer Selection

The most thorough way to pick an answer choice is to identify and eliminate wrong answers until only one is left, then confirm it is the correct answer. Sometimes an answer choice may immediately seem right, but be careful. The test writers will usually put more than one reasonable answer choice on each question, so take a second to read all of them and make sure that the other choices are not equally obvious. As long as you have time left, it is better to read every answer choice than to pick the first one that looks right without checking the others.

✓ Answer Choice Families

An answer choice family consists of two (in rare cases, three) answer choices that are very similar in construction and cannot all be true at the same time. If you see two answer choices that are direct opposites or parallels, one of them is usually the correct answer. For instance, if one answer choice says that quantity x increases and another either says that quantity x decreases (opposite) or says that quantity y increases (parallel), then those answer choices would fall into the same family. An answer choice that doesn't match the construction of the answer choice family is more likely to be incorrect. Most questions will not have answer choice families, but when they do appear, you should be prepared to recognize them.

✓ Eliminate Answers

Eliminate answer choices as soon as you realize they are wrong, but make sure you consider all possibilities. If you are eliminating answer choices and realize that the last one you are left with is also wrong, don't panic. Start over and consider each choice again. There may be something you missed the first time that you will realize on the second pass.

☑ Avoid Fact Traps

Don't be distracted by an answer choice that is factually true but doesn't answer the question. You are looking for the choice that answers the question. Stay focused on what the question is asking for so you don't accidentally pick an answer that is true but incorrect. Always go back to the question and make sure the answer choice you've selected actually answers the question and is not merely a true statement.

☑ Extreme Statements

In general, you should avoid answers that put forth extreme actions as standard practice or proclaim controversial ideas as established fact. An answer choice that states the "process should be used in certain situations, if…" is much more likely to be correct than one that states the "process should be discontinued completely." The first is a calm rational statement and doesn't even make a definitive, uncompromising stance, using a hedge word *if* to provide wiggle room, whereas the second choice is far more extreme.

☑ Benchmark

As you read through the answer choices and you come across one that seems to answer the question well, mentally select that answer choice. This is not your final answer, but it's the one that will help you evaluate the other answer choices. The one that you selected is your benchmark or standard for judging each of the other answer choices. Every other answer choice must be compared to your benchmark. That choice is correct until proven otherwise by another answer choice beating it. If you find a better answer, then that one becomes your new benchmark. Once you've decided that no other choice answers the question as well as your benchmark, you have your final answer.

☑ Predict the Answer

Before you even start looking at the answer choices, it is often best to try to predict the answer. When you come up with the answer on your own, it is easier to avoid distractions and traps because you will know exactly what to look for. The right answer choice is unlikely to be word-for-word what you came up with, but it should be a close match. Even if you are confident that you have the right answer, you should still take the time to read each option before moving on.

General Strategies

☑ Tough Questions

If you are stumped on a problem or it appears too hard or too difficult, don't waste time. Move on! Remember though, if you can quickly check for obviously incorrect answer choices, your chances of guessing correctly are greatly improved. Before you completely give up, at least try to knock out a couple of possible answers. Eliminate what you can and then guess at the remaining answer choices before moving on.

✓ Check Your Work

Since you will probably not know every term listed and the answer to every question, it is important that you get credit for the ones that you do know. Don't miss any questions through careless mistakes. If at all possible, try to take a second to look back over your answer selection and make sure you've selected the correct answer choice and haven't made a costly careless mistake (such as marking an answer choice that you didn't mean to mark). This quick double check should more than pay for itself in caught mistakes for the time it costs.

✓ Pace Yourself

It's easy to be overwhelmed when you're looking at a page full of questions; your mind is confused and full of random thoughts, and the clock is ticking down faster than you would like. Calm down and maintain the pace that you have set for yourself. Especially as you get down to the last few minutes of the test, don't let the small numbers on the clock make you panic. As long as you are on track by monitoring your pace, you are guaranteed to have time for each question.

✓ Don't Rush

It is very easy to make errors when you are in a hurry. Maintaining a fast pace in answering questions is pointless if it makes you miss questions that you would have gotten right otherwise. Test writers like to include distracting information and wrong answers that seem right. Taking a little extra time to avoid careless mistakes can make all the difference in your test score. Find a pace that allows you to be confident in the answers that you select.

✓ Keep Moving

Panicking will not help you pass the test, so do your best to stay calm and keep moving. Taking deep breaths and going through the answer elimination steps you practiced can help to break through a stress barrier and keep your pace.

Final Notes

The combination of a solid foundation of content knowledge and the confidence that comes from practicing your plan for applying that knowledge is the key to maximizing your performance on test day. As your foundation of content knowledge is built up and strengthened, you'll find that the strategies included in this chapter become more and more effective in helping you quickly sift through the distractions and traps of the test to isolate the correct answer.

Now that you're preparing to move forward into the test content chapters of this book, be sure to keep your goal in mind. As you read, think about how you will be able to apply this information on the test. If you've already seen sample questions for the test and you have an idea of the question format and style, try to come up with questions of your own that you can answer based on what you're reading. This will give you valuable practice applying your knowledge in the same ways you can expect to on test day.

Good luck and good studying!

The Process of Auditing Information Systems

ISACA Code of Ethics

According to the Information Systems Audit and Control Association, or ISACA, IS auditors must follow a professional code of ethics. This code, which was created by the ISACA, requires that auditors:

- Help implement the correct policies, standards, procedures, and guidelines.
- Be impartial and professional, perform due diligence, and use best practices.
- Provide accurate information and relevant facts to the correct parties.
- Keep any audit information confidential unless the proper authorities direct otherwise. Auditors should not use any information for personal gain.
- Fulfill stakeholder interests using only legal and honest means.
- Only perform tasks that match their competency level while seeking to expand their competencies.
- Help educate stakeholders about information systems.

If an auditor does not abide by this code, he or she may face legal or punitive action.

Audit Standards

ISACA audit standards are as follows:

- *S1 Audit Charter* – Every audit requires a charter that authorizes its scope and empowers the auditor, who is given authority and responsibility over the audit as well as accountability for its outcome.
- *S2 Independence* – Auditors must be able to prove they are independent, both professionally and organizationally, from the subject of the audit.
- *S3 Professional Ethics and Standards of Conduct* – Auditors must conduct themselves professionally at all times.
- *S4 Professional Competence* – Auditors can only perform tasks for which they are trained, and should increase their competencies through continuing education.
- *S5 Planning* – Preparation is necessary for a successful audit. Proper planning includes establishing objectives and certain a plan for fulfilling objectives.
- *S6 Performance of Audit Work* – The work of auditors must be supervised. This supervision ensures that all conclusions have been documented and are supported by evidence.
- *S7 Audit reporting* – Audit reports must follow ISACA guidelines, and should include required statements and legal disclosures.
- *S8 Follow-up Activities* – Following an audit, auditors will ascertain if management has promptly implemented any suggested changes.

- *S9 Irregularities and Illegal Acts* – Auditors must abide by this standard if they learn that the auditee is performing irregular or illegal activities.
- *S10 IT Governance* – Auditors must analyze the auditee's use of information technology and determine if there is a better, more efficient way he can fulfill his needs.
- *S11 Use of Risk Analysis in Audit Planning* – Using this standard, audit planning incorporates a risk-based approach to planning.

Auditors

An *audit* seeks to provide an unbiased assessment of internal controls by following an established criteria and process, examining past events, and collecting evidence. In addition to giving an impartial opinion of internal controls, auditors must observe a *fiduciary relationship,* which requires the auditor to pursue fairness and honesty above his own interests or the auditee's interests. An auditor should produce verifiable and accurate results, and report only findings supported by his evidence, whether good or bad. Audits are usually accurate when their findings agree with the findings of management. However, a discrepancy between the auditor's opinions and those of management may reveal a need for further analysis.

- *Auditor* – Examines and evaluates internal controls. External auditors should be completely independent from the subject being audited. By following the same standards used in financial auditing, IS auditors can provide impartial assessments while protecting themselves from liability.
- *Auditee* –The subject being audited
- *Independent test* – Determines if the auditor is truly independent from the auditee. In conducting this test, the auditor should determine if any of the following criteria are present:
  - Personal relationship with the auditee
  - Any feelings or conflicts that might affect the audit's outcome
  - Opportunities to benefit, financially or otherwise, from the audit's results
  - Any business, financial, or legal stake in the auditee

If any of these criteria are present, the auditor is not independent and should discontinue the audit.

Auditor Characteristics

Good auditors protect and secure the various documentation and information generated by the audit process. They save and lock important files when they are not being used, and physically secure their laptops. The auditing team should designate a meeting place, such as a *war room*, whose location is remote enough to dissuade and limit eavesdropping from persons not associated with the auditing team. When conducting interviews with such persons, auditors should select a secure area away from the war room. Good communication is essential to good auditing. Auditors should seek to alleviate the auditee's anxiety or trepidation by creating mutual respect. They should address the auditee's concerns and never assign guilt to a specific person for a mistake; rather, they should validate the auditee's feelings, provide reassurance, and suggest a different course of action. Auditors should be always respectful and never insulting.

Leadership Qualities and Vetting

An auditor must set specific responsibilities for team members and assume accountability for the audit's outcome. He should create a workplace atmosphere in which the audit team is comfortable asking questions, making suggestions, and offering criticism. Team members should be able to differentiate between the auditor's mandatory directives and his discretionary ones. We should note that good leadership is about more than giving orders. It is also about planning, prioritizing, handling conflict, imparting vision, inspiring subordinates, and convincing them of the validity and necessity of project goals. Inspired workers are more likely to produce good results than disinterested workers. When conducting interviews with clients, auditors will utilize the process of *vetting*; this analyzes and edits words as a means of furthering audit goals.

External vs. Internal Auditors

External auditors must be completely independent from the auditee. Their job is to provide an unbiased view of an organization's internal controls; therefore, they should have no stake—financial, personal, or otherwise—in the organization or the outcome of the audit. *Internal auditors* come from within the organization. They cannot be considered independent or external, because they work for the auditee. However, they do serve a number of important purposes. For instance, if the organization has an upcoming external audit, internal auditors can assume a role of independence and assist the organization as it prepares for external auditors. Or, if an organization is experiencing problems from its internal controls, internal auditors may be able to remedy those problems far less expensively than external auditors.

Types of Audits

Recommended vs. Required Regulations

Each audit goal should be justified by a specific ISACA standard or regulation. By referencing and citing these standards, auditors can help clients understand the purpose of every activity undertaken during the audit. *Recommended regulations* are discretionary and are normally accompanied by the verb *should. Required regulations*, on the other hand, are mandatory and are normally accompanied by the verb *shall.* Organizations must comply with required regulations even if they stand to lose money; otherwise, they may face severe punitive measures, such as heavy fines and expulsion from the industry. Compliance with required regulations should be a top priority for any auditor. Courts very rarely excuse cases of noncompliance.

Audits fall into two basic categories: compliance and substantive. *Compliance tests* ensure compliance with applicable standards and regulations. *Substantive tests* determine the veracity of a management claim. The exam may feature the following types of audits:

- *Compliance audit* – Ensures the client is following and implementing all applicable rules and regulations (such as federal laws, ISO standards, or other organizational standards) by determining the kinds of controls in place.
- *Administrative audit* – Ensures the client has created and implemented a set of policies and procedures by testing for required documentation.
- *Financial audit* – Determines whether or not an organization's accounting methods conform to accepted accounting methods. Financial audits examine a client's balances and financial records.
- *Operational audit* – Ensures the client is using the most efficient operational processes possible. These types of audits follow the Statement of Account Standard 70, or SAS-70, and are especially prevalent in process and service areas.
- *Integrated audit* – Examines financial and operation controls, and follows SAS-94 standard.
- *Information systems audit* – Ensures that systems meet a certain certification or accreditation. Certifications are achieved by fulfilling objective reference standards. Accreditations, however, involve fulfilling management's standards.

Performance Reviews

Performance reviews involve monitoring and tracking a process's compliance to internal controls. Auditors use performance reviews to determine any compliance issues that require remediation. Outsourcing contracts often include concessions intended to coerce one party into signing. When evaluating outsourcing contracts, auditors should consider the concessions offered by their clients. Concessions may include the following:

- Specialized personnel who are no longer at the client's location
- Knowledge, materials, or techniques
- Contract change cost
- Possibility of contract cancellation

In the event of contract cancellation, auditors must consider the resources necessary to find a replacement.

Executive Performance Review

During an executive performance review, the audit committee evaluates the executive staff and the validity of its assumptions. The review should provide internal control solutions and a framework in which executives can discuss sensitive information. In order to obtain an impartial opinion on executive management and internal controls, the committee may hire an independent auditor, who should verify the existence of IT governance and an IT strategy. The auditor should examine the performance, plans, and meeting minutes of the steering committee, the CEO, and executives. He should also ensure that any IT strategy is founded on sound business objectives.

Capability Maturity Model

The Capability Maturity Model, or CMM, is a type of performance review. It assesses the maturity of a process, meaning the process's ability to be controlled and continuously improved. The CMM rates processes according to the following levels:

- *Level 0: Nothing* – Processes are missing.
- *Level 1: Initial* – Processes exist, but are disorganized. They can only generate acceptable outputs if personnel and resources surpass their capabilities.
- *Level 2: Repeatable* – Processes can be repeated, tracked, and described using a WBS. Process documentation includes basic standards, descriptions, and procedures.
- *Level 3: Defined* – Management can predict process outcome using qualitative measures, and the documentation set expands to include additional standards, measurements, objectives, and improvement procedures.
- *Level 4: Managed* – Management can predict process outcome using quantitative measures. Processes are controlled and improved using measurement criteria.
- *Level 5: Optimized* – Processes are continuously improved and revised as business objectives and requirements change.

Tactical Management and Benchmarking

Tactical management evaluates IS results by gathering performance metrics and comparing them against a baseline. The purpose of tactical management is improving IS performance, controlling investment return on information systems, and supporting strategic objectives. Managers must first decide on a set of metrics as well as a means of collecting those metrics, which will also be used to convey data to stakeholders. *Benchmarking* compares the IS results of an organization against some industry standard, such as the Federal Information Security Management Act or the National Institute of Standards and Technology. Auditors use benchmarking to optimize IS performance, and to evaluate the organization using standards that are universal to the industry. Organizations often create their business and contingency plans using benchmarks such as Business Continuity Maturity Model and Capability Maturity Model.

Legal Aspects

Sarbanes-Oxley Act of 2002

The Sarbanes-Oxley Act of 2002, or SOX, requires that management disclose internal control information. According to *Act 906* of SOX, management must confirm the veracity and completeness of its financial records. Also, according to *Act 302* of SOX, management must make full disclosure of internal controls to the audit committee. Full disclosure includes any deficiencies or weaknesses. With SOX, the government can more easily identify and prosecute those organizations that provide faulty or misleading information.

Confidentiality and Least Privilege

Auditors are often privy to information that could be very damaging to a client if disclosed publicly; therefore, maintaining confidentiality is one of the most important tasks of auditing. Auditors should never take sensitive information from the client's office. In the event that an auditor discovers illegal activities, he should seek legal counsel regarding confidentiality and disclosure laws before contacting the authorities. He should also observe the practice of least privilege in all situations. *Least privilege* involves disclosing as little information as necessary to fulfill a certain task. All information pertaining to an audit will be stored in a document file archive, which should remain with the client unless illegal activities are discovered. Auditors should backup, support, and protect audit documents (working papers, templates, spreadsheets, etc.) using the latest technology and security devices.

Audit Components and Stages

Every audit contains ten stages:

1. Obtain approval for the audit charter or engagement letter.
2. Preplan the audit.
3. Conduct a risk assessment.
4. Evaluate the feasibility of an audit (i.e., determine whether an audit is even possible).
5. Collect evidence.
6. Perform compliance tests.
7. Perform substantive tests.
8. Analyze evidence and test results.
9. Report findings and auditor's opinion.
10. Carry out follow-up procedures.

Scheduling Activities and Diagramming

Schedule activities are the actions that must be undertaken to fulfill project processes and goals. Project management illustrates the relationships between schedule activities using various *diagramming techniques.* One common type of diagram is a *Gantt chart,* which represents each schedule activity as a bar. Longer bars denote longer activities, and vice versa. Sequential activities are arranged horizontally, while concurrent activities are arranged vertically. Another common type of diagram is a *Programmed Evaluation Review Technique (PERT) diagram,* which arranges activities along a series of pathways. Because certain activities must be completed before other activities can begin, each pathway arranges activities in the order they must be performed, and includes a duration time for each activity.

The longest pathway through a PERT diagram is known as the *critical path,* which represents the least amount of time in which the project can be completed.

AUDIT COMMITTEES

Audit committees consist of business executives, and assist the executive accounting officer as he manages the organization's internal controls. Audit committees exist within every organization, and have the following responsibilities:

- Advising executives on strategy
- Analyzing and disputing an executive's assurance about internal controls
- Issuing and approving charters for internal audits
- Issuing and approving engagement letters for external audits
- Overseeing audit activities

PREPLANNING

Preplanning is the process of determining the actions and tasks necessary to fulfill audit objectives, and involves following a set of professional auditing standards and legal guidelines. If an auditor ignores established auditing procedures, he must justify doing so. Organizations should revise their own preplanning procedures on a yearly basis in order to incorporate new techniques and technologies. As part of preplanning, auditors should understand the audit's impact on the business by examining the following business-related factors:

- Business operations (Industry regulations; organizational processes and business and reporting cycles; etc.)
- Strategic objectives (IS plans, expectations, and goals; strategic plans; tactical plans; work in progress; etc.)
- Financial objectives (ROI for capital investment and other expenses; cost allocation, budgeting, and forecasting; SOX requirements; asset management; etc.)

Internal controls operational objectives (type of audit; staffing plans; controls for network communications; recovery plans; performance measurements; system administration; etc.)

AUDIT CHARTER

Audits cannot be performed without an audit charter, which authorizes the audit, fully explains its goals and objectives, and comprises the first stage of the audit process. Audit charters are approved by the highest levels of the organization (board of directors or executive management) as well as the audit committee, and detail the following information:

- *Authority* – Empowers the auditor to perform the audit and to access all necessary information.
- *Responsibility* – Explains the audit's scope, including its objectives.
- *Accountability* – Defines the relationship between auditor and audit committee.

Engagement Letters

Organizations use engagement letters when procuring an independent audit from an external third party. Engagement letters are part of the audit charter, but establish the auditor's independence from the procuring organization while documenting the specifics of their relationship. Engagement letters contain the following information:

- Statement of auditor's independence
- Reiteration of all information explained in the project charter
- Explanation of terms and conditions between the independent auditor and the audit committee
- Audit completion dates

Risk Assessment

Risk assessment involves identifying and documenting potential risks to the auditee. Auditors cannot properly evaluate risk without access to the following information: protected assets; potential threats to assets; exposures for assets; possible sources of threats, both external and internal to the organization; and unresolved security problems. Once potential risks have become known, the auditor will select the most appropriate response strategy:

- *Avoidance* – Alter project conditions to eliminate the risk
- *Transference* – Allocate the impact of the risk event to a third party, usually by contracting out or purchasing insurance. The auditor still bears responsibility for audit failure, however.
- *Mitigation* – Lessen the impact of a risk event if it occurs, usually through internal controls
- *Acceptance* – Simply allow the risk event to occur. Certain risks may admit no other option.

The auditee should assist the auditor as he performs the risk assessment. If the auditee is unwilling to provide the necessary information, an audit may not be possible.

A *risk event* is any event capable of impacting organizational assets either directly or indirectly, such as theft, fraud, implementing faulty controls or procedures, etc. *Risk* is the probability that such an event will occur. Risk events can have both positive and negative impacts, but auditors are mainly concerned with negative risks, or *threats.* Threats can damage organizational assets, such as buildings, documents, information, materials, and goods or services. *Personnel risks* are associated with hiring and firing employees. This kind of risk is especially important when an organization has outsourced to an offshore location where a series of layoffs may incur more expenses than they would have in the US, such as larger severance packages, medical cost, relocation of the former employee, etc. *Information security risks* are associated with data security. For instance, when an organization engages in outsourcing, it may be transferring sensitive data through mediums that are not as secure as they would be in the US.

Types of Risk

Auditors may encounter the following types of risk:

- *Inherent risks* – Innate to the subject of the audit. These are always present, such as the risk of hurricane damage to a structure on the coastline.
- *Business risks* – Financial, contractual, or regulatory risks that are innate to the business or industry.
- *Detection risks* – The dangers that cause an auditor to miss a crucial piece of evidence or overlook an important condition to the audit. There are two types of detection risk: *Sampling risk,* which is the chance that an auditor will accept bad evidence or dismiss good evidence, and *Nonsampling risk,* which is the chance that an auditor will misapply audit procedures and overlook an important condition.
- *Audit risks* – The result of detection, inherent, control, and residual risks working in conjunction.
- *Control risks* – Realized when an auditor loses control over the audit, and may result in problems that are never corrected.
- *Technological risks* – Inherent to automation and technology.
- *Operational* risks – The chances that a process will not work as intended.
- *Residual risks* – Any risks that remain after all mitigation efforts have been exhausted.

Monetary Loss Calculations

The following formula calculates the monetary loss incurred by a single occurrence of a particular risk event:

$$\text{asset value in dollars} \times \text{exposure factor as a percentage} = \text{single loss expectancy}$$

$$(\text{AV} \times \text{EF} = \text{SLE})$$

Using the SLE, an auditor can estimate an annual loss for the risk with the following formula:

$$\text{single loss expectancy} \times \text{annual rate of occurrence} = \text{annual loss expectancy}$$

$$(\text{SLE} \times \text{ARO} = \text{ALE})$$

Consider a building worth $1 million. If the building sustains weather damage equaling 1% of its total worth, the SLE would be calculated:

$$AV \times EF = SLE$$

$$\$1 \text{ million} \times .01 = \$10{,}000$$

If such weather conditions occur 3 times a year, the annual loss expectancy would be calculated:

$$SLE \times ARO = ALE$$

$$\$10{,}000 \times 3 = \$30{,}000$$

Feasibility

Before gathering evidence or performing tests, auditors must determine the feasibility of an audit. In doing so, auditors are often required to examine activities that their clients (the auditees) have outsourced to a third-party vendor. In these cases, the client still remains liable for the success or failure of the activity even though it has been contracted out. Third parties can hinder or even stop an audit if they refuse to be audited; therefore, the outsourcing contract should include a *right to audit* stipulation. In response to audit requests, many third-party vendors simply send out an *SAS-70 report.* Auditors, however, should be wary of these reports, because they may not contain all necessary information and may even misrepresent important pieces of evidence. Regardless of circumstance, clients and auditors must cooperate closely when a third party is involved.

Internal Controls

Internal controls include the policies, procedures, and best practices of an organization, and are designed to detect, limit, and prevent risk events from affecting business objectives. Internal controls are categorized according to three groups:

- *Preventive controls* avoid the risk event entirely. For instance, by requiring authorization to access certain information, an organization can prevent a security leak before it even occurs. Although preventive controls are the most effective deterrent to risk, they may not be the most cost efficient.
- *Detective controls* find risks as they become known, and inform the organization that action may be required in order to avoid consequences. For instance, a detective control would alert the organization if an unauthorized user has accessed crucial information.
- *Corrective (or reactive) controls* correct issues after the risk event has occurred. For instance, if the unauthorized user deleted important files, a corrective control might implement a recovery program to restore the lost information.

Compliance Testing

Compliance testing determines whether a particular control is present or absent. Specifically, it ensures that procedures are being properly implemented, and that controls such as access rights and system audits logs are being used. Compliance testing uses these sampling techniques:

- *Discovery* – Utilized when evidence is scarce and the auditor's goal is to determine fraud.
- *Stop-and-go* – Allows the acquisition of samples with a minimal amount of effort. This technique enables the auditor to discontinue testing as early as possible, and is only used when a sample is expected to contain few errors.
- *Attribute* – Determines how often a control is absent or present in a sample. For instance, if a control is absent once in a sample size of 25, the attribute sample would be 25 percent.
- *Precision (or expected error) rate* – Determines if the margin of error between the audit sample and the entire population is within acceptable margins. Precision rate is calculated as a percentage.

Implementation Methods

Each type of internal control (preventive, detective, and corrective/reactive) can be implemented using three different methods:

- *The administrative method* involves policies, procedures, and standards. Preventive examples include a company's hiring practices. Detective examples include risk assessments and data checks. Corrective examples include information recovery plans and lessons learned.
- *The physical method* incorporates physical obstacles. Preventive examples include walls and security guards. Detective examples include receipts and physical signs (finger prints, broken locks) of a break in. Corrective examples include climate control devices and fire sprinklers.
- *The technical method* involves technological barriers, such as computer programs. Preventive examples include anti-virus software and access codes. Detective examples include identification software and intruder detection systems. Corrective examples include data-recovery software and redundancy failsafe systems.

Evidence

Collecting Evidence

Auditors use the following techniques when collecting evidence:

- *Interviews* should be performed in a timely manner, so that the auditor can discuss any relevant topics broached by the interviewee. Auditors should use the interviewee's facial responses and body language as a means of determining which issues require further examination. Interviews should feature only persons and questions relevant to the audit's objectives.

- *Observation* normally involves watching personnel as they go about their daily work and activities.
- *Surveys* are less time consuming than an interview, but lack the advantages of an interview; auditors cannot gauge the physical reactions of the interviewee or explore topics.
- *Documentation review* entails the examination of existing documents, such as contracts, laws, and other legal records.
- *Workshops* take the place of individual interviews in some cases. Auditors address a group of people, such as the audit committee, and help them better understand the audit's purpose and objectives.

Direct and Indirect Evidence

Evidence is classified in two main categories: direct evidence and indirect evidence. *Direct evidence* is any written documentation or eyewitness account, and is considered concrete proof of a fact. *Indirect (or circumstantial) evidence* relies on inference, which is a reasonable supposition drawn from a known truth; essentially, an auditor reaches a hypothesis based on the logical progression of events. In practice, an auditor prefers direct evidence because indirect evidence is far less tangible. A high level of reliance on indirect evidence normally invalidates an audit.

Evidence Timing

Evidence timing describes the promptness of evidence retrieval. It determines if the evidence has arrived in a timely manner or, in regards to electronic data, if the required evidence has been deleted or overwritten. Evidence timing is another important consideration for the auditor.

Material Relevance and Objectivity

Evidence is graded according to material relevance and objectivity. Evidence possesses material relevance if it changes the auditor's findings, meaning the auditor would have reached a different conclusion if the evidence had been absent. Material relevance implies that the evidence correlates strongly and logically to the issues and concerns of the audit. Objective evidence possesses an obvious and unbiased factual nature, and requires very little judgment or explanation. If an auditor must explain why a particular piece of evidence should be accepted as fact, the evidence is likely not objective. Objective evidence is obtained and verified through testing, observation, and documentation.

Independence and Competency of Source

Evidence is graded according to independence and competence of evidence source.

The persons or sources providing the evidence should be completely independent from the auditee. They should have no stake in the organization being audited, and should receive no benefit from the evidence becoming known. A person is more likely to provide good evidence if he has expertise in the subject matter. Experts can draw conclusions or notice details that non-experts might miss. Additionally, a person who is experienced in evidence collection will likely formulate better opinions and gather more relevant data than an inexperienced person. Although auditors prefer evidence from sources working directly in the audit process, they should not simply dismiss more distantly associated testimony, which may provide new insight.

EVIDENCE LIFE CYCLE

The *evidence life cycle* consists of seven phases: identification, collection, initial preservation storage, analysis, post analysis preservation storage, presentation, and return to owner. Collectively, these phases are known as the *chain of custody*. Each piece of evidence must be subjected to all phases; otherwise, the auditor risks mishandling the evidence and incurring legal action. In fact, an audit invites tampering charges if evidence does not go through the entire chain of custody.

- The *identification phase* involves labeling, dating, and tagging evidence immediately following its discovery, for purposes of tracking. Tags should include a brief summary of the evidence's relevance. Also, auditors should document the location and condition of the evidence when it was discovered. Proper identification helps ensure that evidence is not lost as it is gathered.
- During the *collection phase*, a custodian collects and secures evidence. The custodian may need to exercise additional care with highly valuable or confidential items. This is especially true for records and documents, which, if possible, should not be removed from the auditee's premises.
- The goal of the *initial preservation storage phase* is maintaining evidence in the same condition it was found. This phase prevents alteration to the evidence, and protects auditors and custodians against accusations of tampering.
- During the *analysis phase,* evidence is subjected to various kinds of testing—qualitative measurement, quantitative measurement, observation, etc. Auditors must document all test results, and re-perform tests when necessary. If a test result is particularly unusual, the auditor may seek a third-party tester to corroborate the finding.
- The *post-analysis preservation storage phase* involves returning evidence to storage after it has been analyzed. The storage facility should both secure and preserve the evidence, and it should only be removed for retesting and presentation. Any alteration or damage invites legal action and accusations of tampering.
- During the *presentation phase,* the auditor creates and presents his report along with any supporting evidence. Reports include a level of detail determined by the type and subject of the audit. For instance, reports involving criminal cases require a substantial amount of detail.
- The *return to owner phase* is performed after the audit is concluded. As expected, the client reassumes possession of the evidence. In most situations, evidence is returned as soon as the audit is completed; however, if criminal activity is suspected, evidence may be held for years.

SUBSTANTIVE TESTING

Substantive testing determines if the actual state of the evidence coincides with management claims about the evidence. For instance, it may evaluate the performance of a process, or count client inventory. Substantive testing estimates a total for a group of related items or persons using the following sampling techniques:

- *Variable* – Uses the characteristics of a sample (e.g., weight) to extrapolate the worth of an entire population, such as an inventory. For instance, consider an item worth $2 that weighs 1 pound. If the entire population of that item weighs 100 pounds, we can calculate a total population worth of $200.
- *Stratified mean estimation* – Separates a large population into smaller demographic groups according to some characteristic, such as gender, age, etc. Its goal is formulating an average for each group.
- *Unstratified mean estimation* – Seeks to estimate a total for the entire population.
- *Different estimation* – Calculates the value difference between claims that have been audited and those that have not been audited.
- *Tolerable error rate* – Determines the maximum amount of errors that can exist before management's claims are considered invalid.

EVIDENCE AND MATERIALITY

Evidence is any verifiable information gathered by the auditor, and is used to either corroborate or disprove a particular point. It enables the auditor to substantiate a claim of management, reach an opinion, and fulfill audit goals. Evidence can include policies and procedures, interviews, observations, previous audit results, test results, financial documents, business plans, emails, and many other forms of documentation. Auditors must have sufficient, reliable evidence before they create an *auditor's opinion*, and all opinions should be supported by verifiable evidence. Good evidence is generally self-explanatory and requires little commentary. If the auditor finds himself constantly explaining and justifying the validity of the evidence, his evidence is most likely poor. When examining evidence, an auditor should consider its *materiality,* which describes the evidence's importance in validating audit goals and its ability to alter the audit's outcome.

RELIABLE EVIDENCE

Reliable evidence possesses the following characteristics:

- *Independence from the auditee* – When an auditor obtains evidence from a source external to the auditee, he can be assured of its reliability and trustworthiness. Sources are only considered independent if they have no stake in the auditee.

- *Qualified and dependable source* – The person providing the evidence must be dependable and possess the necessary qualifications. Similarly, the auditor must be qualified in the subject of the audit; otherwise, he may miss key test results or misinterpret evidence.
- *Objectivity* – Evidence possessing a higher level of objectivity tends to be more reliable. Generally speaking, tests generate more objective evidence than interviews.
- *Good timing* – Organizational practices and procedures often affect when evidence comes available. Unfortunately, these practices and procedures do not always coincide with the auditing schedule.

Audit Documentation

Audit documentation is created and prepared throughout the audit's lifetime. It should do the following: explain the audit's purpose; identify all persons involved; document the subject of the audit; detail the methods for acquiring evidence and testing; list the audit's time and location; and finally, explain how the audit was carried out. In the early stages of the audit, documentation consists of duplicates of the audit charter, scope, policies, procedures, and plans. As the audit moves forward, the documentation set expands to include the auditor's working notes, final papers, and duplicates of any reports. Auditors should be meticulous record keepers, because their findings may be required in the future. Future auditors should be able to recreate the findings of the current audit by following its paperwork. The retention period for documentation varies depending on the type of audit. For instance, integrated audits retain their records for at least seven years.

Document Types

The following kinds of documents:

- *Policies* document specific organizational objectives. Policies are high-level documents that carry mandatory compliance. They are integral to the functioning of an organization, and are approved by the senior high-ranking corporate official.
- *Standards* guarantee that organizational members are conforming to policies. Standards are mid-level documents, carry a mandatory compliance, and usually require testing or auditing of processes. They are approved by management.
- *Guidelines* suggest methods for meeting company policies in the absence of standards. Guidelines are discretionary, and include information about meeting company goals and performing other activities that might prove helpful to the organization.
- *Procedures* control project outcomes by ensuring that standards are fulfilled. Procedures normally include a series of required activities and troubleshooting tips. They carry mandatory compliance, and may be updated or changed if they prove to be ineffective.

Audit Samples

Before conducting any tests, auditors must select *audit samples* using the following methods: statistical sampling and nonstatistical sampling. *Statistical sampling* relies on objective mathematical formulas and expresses the sample as a percentage. There are a few notable ways to arrive at a statistical sample: *random sampling*, which uses random selection; *cell sampling*, which makes a selection at predetermined intervals; and, *fixed-interval sampling*, which makes a selection using a formula. A less objective method is *nonstatistical sampling*, also known as *judgmental sampling*. It relies on the auditor's personal judgment to determine the sample selection method and set the sample size. One type of nonstatistical sampling is *haphazard sampling*, which randomly makes a selection. Regardless of the sampling method used, auditors should be wary of *sampling risk*, in which a faulty conclusion is reached because of poor sampling.

Auditor's Final Report

Following the audit's completion, the auditor must present his findings to the auditee and management. This presentation should include the following information:

- Audit's scope and objectives
- Actual work performed
- Dates covered by the audit
- Research methodology and procedures
- Audit results, detailed findings, and their implications
- Any restrictions or limitations on the audit process and final report
- Auditor's opinion, if the findings warrant it.

This presentation will be included in a *final report*, which contains all of the aforementioned information as well as the following: a statement of independence, usually in the title; executive summary; displays, such as graphs and charts; audit standards; all parties involved in the audit; whether or not those parties reach consensus on the research methodology and procedures; all necessary disclaimers and statements; working notes; and auditor's approval (signature).

After Final Report

- *Exit interviews* are conducted after the auditor has submitted the final report. During these interviews, the auditor and auditee discuss the methods by which management will implement the auditor's suggestions, and establish an estimated time frame. The purpose of exit interviews is to elicit a commitment from the auditee. If the auditor discovers he has omitted certain necessary procedures after the audit, he may need to alter or even rewrite the final report. He may even invite legal action if the omissions alter the audit's outcome.

- *Follow-up activities* address any issues arising after the audit. These issues may invalidate some findings in the final reports, and can be classified into two categories: *Type 1 events* describe issues discovered before the balance sheet date. *Type 2 events* describe issues discovered following the balance sheet date.

Illegal Activities

Auditors may uncover the following types of illegal activities:

- *Regulatory infractions* – Occur when a person knowingly or unknowingly breaks the law.
- *Theft (also known as conversion)* – Includes activities such as embezzlement, wherein a person obtains resources that do not belong to him.
- *Fraud* – Involves using deception or misrepresentation for one's own benefit.
- *Suppression* – Occurs when an organization holds back documents or records that may reflect poorly on its transactions. Obstruction and willful omission are examples of suppression.
- *Racketeering* – Involves repeatedly committing illegal activities, specifically fraud. Racketeering laws are part of the Racketeer Influenced and Corrupt Organization Act, or RICO.

Auditors should suspect the presence of these activities if clients exhibit any of the following characteristics: poor record keeping; excessively high, excessively low, or unexplained payments; and, questionable record keeping.

Proper Response When Illegal Activity Is Discovered

The audit plan will explain the specific actions an auditor should undertake upon discovering illegal activities. In addition to the audit plan, auditors should also follow these responses:

- Document any evidence of illegal activity.
- Determine the extent of the auditee's involvement – i.e., whether he is an unaware or willing accomplice.
- Examine any conditions that may have caused management to misrepresent its claims.
- Acquire legal advice, especially concerning disclosure laws, so the auditor avoids implication in illegal doings. In fact, auditors should only inform law officers if legal counsel advises them to do so.
- Inform higher-level management if the activities are constrained to a lower level of management. Auditors should inform the highest level of management if the persons associated with the activities are part of internal controls.

Governance and Management of IT

Information Systems

Every information system includes three standard roles:

- *Data Owner* – Assumes responsibility for the veracity and accuracy of information. He admits or rejects access to data, establishes controls, and appoints the custodian.
- *Data User* – Is empowered to use the system and its information, but must abide by usage requirements. He helps preserve security by reporting any system misuses.
- *Data Custodian* – Supports users by making information available. He safeguards the data and the system, enforces controls, and fulfills tasks related to independent audits.

Anyone performing the above tasks, regardless of whether or not he works in the IT department, is considered to be in the role. The audit's goals and objectives determine who the auditor must interview, but identifying the persons (or person) responsible for the above roles is very important to the interview process.

Corporate Positions

The following corporate positions:

- *Board of directors* consists of people who have a vested monetary interest in the corporation, such as investors or advisers. They seldom involve themselves in the corporation's daily workings; instead, they advise CEOs and CFOs. Although board members are normally absolved from liability, the government can prosecute them when the situation warrants it.
- *Chief executive officer*, or *CEO*, guides the organization and devises business strategy. His main pursuit is generating profit for the organization, and he does so by finding new buyers. Like all corporate officers, CEOs have signing authority and can be prosecuted by the government.
- *Chief financial officer*, or CFO, directs the controls over IS, human resources, accounting, and capital. CFOs also have liability.
- *Chief information officer*, or CIO, works under and reports to the CFO. CIOs may or may not be actual corporate officers; therefore, their liability status is uncertain. It is contingent upon the corporation.
- *President or general manager* leads the business division. He is a corporate officer and subject to legal liability. One goal of the SOX Act is increasing the liability of officers; therefore, SOX suggests that a company make all presidents and general managers sign integrity statements.
- *Vice president* is behind only the president in the business division chain of command. He is a corporate officer and subject to government prosecution.

- *Department directors* include upper management, and may include minor and major levels depending on the company's size. They are not corporate officers.
- *Managers and staff workers* oversee and manage staff members on a daily basis. The government will only prosecute managers and staff workers if they have willfully engaged in criminal acts.

Audit Firm Positions

The following audit firm positions:

- *Partner* leads the audit firm with a primary focus on creating profit. His responsibilities include representing the firm, seeking out new executive clients, supporting various management functions, and training new staff. In most cases, partners agree to generate $15 million annually for their respective firms.
- *Engagement managers* are responsible for executing the audit, leading the audit staff, and handling clients.
- *Senior consultants* manage the day-to-day operations of the audit and the audit staff. They lend insight and analysis while working with the client staff.
- *Consultants* perform audit objectives while working directly with the client. They should need a minimal amount of supervision.
- *Systems analyst* is the lowest in the organizational hierarchy; it is normally an entry-level position. These individuals perform low-level work while gaining experience.

Projects vs. Audits

The characteristics of IS audits are very similar to those of projects; therefore, auditors should have a thorough understand of the components of a project. All *projects* possess the following qualities:

- *Impermanence* – Projects are not part of an organization's permanent, ongoing functions; therefore, they must have definite start and finish dates. Although organizations perform audits on a regular basis, each audit has its own scope and set of goals, which must be started and completed at specific times.
- *Uniqueness* – The goal of any project is generating a specific and unique good or service. Similarly, an audit always produces unique information, even though it follows the same process that other audits follow.
- *Progressive elaboration* – As the project (or audit) moves forward, members of the project team gain a better understanding of the purposes and possible applications. This information is then integrated into project (or audit) management and definition processes.

SECURITY AUDITS

Auditors should meet the following competencies before conducting a security audit:

- General management skills
- Communication skills
- Knowledge and certifications pertaining to security audits
- Understanding of the specific functional area that is the subject of the audit
- Understanding of the specific processes and procedures used by the organization being audited

These competencies are rooted in the standards of the *Project Management Institute,* or *PMI,* which is an organization dedicated to identifying and explaining the 44 processes of project management. PMI standards are found in many areas of auditing, and serve as guidelines against which auditors can evaluate their own processes.

STRATEGY AND CORPORATE GOVERNANCE

A *strategy is* a detailed, systematic plan that adapts some behavior or structure. Organizational executives ensure proper *corporate governance* by treating shareholders in an ethical manner and, thereby, receiving the maximum possible returns on financial investments. Organizations will not be successful unless they define and implement strategy using sound corporate governance. Auditors facilitate corporate governance and strategy implementation by validating the following management objectives:

- Use of assurance practices
- Planning intended to align IT and business objectives
- Verifying the proper functioning of internal controls, which facilitate the implementation of strategy.

PERSONS INVOLVED IN MAKING AND APPROVING IT STRATEGY

IT strategy is created and approved by executive management, such as the CEO, CFO, COO, Project Sponsor, and the IT Steering Committee. The strategy is then sent down to the CIO and the Vice President of Information Technology for approval. Executive management must also choose one of the following methods for funding the strategy:

- *Shared cost* – Every organizational member and department assumes some share of IT costs. Although this is an efficient method of payment, it may lead to discontentment among members who feel they are not benefiting from the system.

- *Sponsor pays* – The sponsor agrees to pay for all IT costs in exchange for increased power over the decision-making process. This method tends to create power struggles over IT management.
- *Charge-back* – departments and members are only charged when they use IT systems.

Data and Technology Plans

An IT strategy plan helps carry out organizational objectives, and supports a specific company goal. For instance, if the goal is increasing the security level around company assets, a corresponding IT plan may involve creating better security systems. There are multiple types of IT strategy plans, including the following:

- *Data plans* set forth the manner in which data will be used. For instance, after the organization has determined a use for marketing data, it will create a system for managing that data.
- *Technology plans* set forth the hardware and software requirements of the organization. As a general rule, an organization should create its technology plan after its data and application management plans; otherwise, it may be forcing incompatible data requirements into its technology.

Types of IT Strategy Plans

- *Application management plans* – Explain the types of work that must be carried out by computer software, and the types of software necessary to complete that work. Organizations will use software that gives them the greatest advantage against their industry competitors, who will likely have similar informational needs.
- *Facilities plans* – Identify where the technology will be located and who will manage it. They also explain the method for acquisitioning technology (outsource, within the organization, some combination thereof, etc.)
- *Organizational plans* – Explains the hierarchical structure of the IT organization, such as the relationships between the CEO, Vice President of IT, CFO, etc.

IT Steering Committee

The *IT steering committee,* also known as the *IT strategy committee,* is responsible for communicating business objectives (as developed by business executives) to the IT executive. Its primary concern is high-level objectives, not the organization's daily operations. The committee is created via a formal charter, and helps align IT and business goals. The charter empowers the committee, grants formal controls, and explains the authority and responsibilities of each member, all of whom should hold a position of at least vice president. Although an executive chairperson oversees the committee, the CEO is actually in charge. He locates sources of potential profit that the committee explores. The CEO can give his directives personally or through a representative. IT committees identify opportunities and make recommendations, often relying on the observations of experts in a particular field. These recommendations must be approved by the board of directors, but the steering committee has the final say in the project's launch.

DEPARTMENTS ON THE IT STEERING COMMITTEE

The IT Steering Committee includes high-ranking representatives from the following departments:

- *Marketing* – Responsible for attracting buyers to the organization's goods or services
- *Sales* – Seeks to increase the number of closed sales using technology
- *Manufacturing/Software development* – Provides information that helps coordinate production and sales
- *Information technology* – Coordinates communication between IT Steering Committee members and the IT organization; either the IT vice president or the CIO fills this liaison role
- *Human resources* – Ensures compliance with federal labor laws, and facilitates personnel management
- *Labor management* – A committee position filled by a member of a labor union or similar organization

ROLES OF THE FOLLOWING DEPARTMENTS ON THE IT STEERING COMMITTEE:

The IT Steering Committee includes high-ranking representatives from the following departments:

- *Research and development* – Improves current goods or services, and develops new ones; the goal of new products is to create profit for at least the next 6 months
- *Finance* – Provides financial and budgetary expertise, and helps receive approval for projects
- *Legal* – Provides legal advice, makes certain that the company is following all necessary laws, and protects the company against liability and risk
- *Quality control* – Ensures the company is following quality standards; in doing so, it can avoid inconsistent production and legal problems
- *Administration* – Keeps records, perform bookkeeping, and processes paperwork
- *Project management* – Informs on existing and future projects

IT GOVERNANCE

Proper IT governance involves creating and implementing a set of formalized policies and procedures designed to mitigate, avoid, or transfer risk events. When evaluating IT governance, auditors should ensure that policies exist for the following business-related components: data integrity, intellectual property, monitoring, incident response, mandatory controls, and discretionary controls. The following are definitions of IT governance terms:

- *Data integrity* involves accurately processing and securely storing data. Specifically, auditors should ensure that existing IT controls perform the following tasks: verify data accuracy; make certain the proper certifications for review are in place; and evaluate the level of security controls. Data integrity should include systems for *backup and restoration* (which help re-sort data in the event of its loss) and *security management* (which restricts access to internal controls).
- *Intellectual property* includes information known only to the organization. Because such information is valuable, the organization should implement IT procedures to protect it.
- *Monitoring* ensures the IT system is aligned with business objectives by using a set of metrics.
- *Incident responses* are necessary when internal controls fail, or technical problems arise. Response teams are trained to evaluate problematic situations and implement a response using the appropriate policies and standards. Response teams should be careful not to mishandle evidence, especially if the problem is criminal in nature; otherwise, the organization may incur legal liability.
- *Mandatory controls* must be implemented, regardless of circumstance. These are the strongest controls, and are applied at both the administrative and technical levels.
- *Discretionary controls* are implemented at the user's judgment and within levels determined by him. These are the weakest controls.

Human Resource Policies

Auditors should verify that the following HR policies fulfill their intended functions:

- *Hiring policies* help the organization conduct an effective interview and choose the right applicant while following any applicable equal opportunity laws.
- *Termination policies* lay out all the situations in which an employee may be let go, as well as the procedures governing those situations. For instance, termination policies often include specific procedures for retirement, layoffs, releasing and recalling contract employees, friendly terminations, and hostile terminations.
- *Corrective counseling policies* help remediate the substandard performance of an employee. If these policies are not implemented properly and the employee is terminated, he may be able to pursue legal action against the organization due to wrongful termination.

- *Performance evaluations* review an employee's performance using set criteria, against which all employees in the same role are measured. Managers should perform evaluations on at least an annual basis, and HR should keep evaluations on file for several years.
- *Promotion policies* should give every employee an opportunity for promotion using objective and nondiscriminatory criteria that fulfill equal opportunity laws.
- *Employee contracts* lay out the terms of employment, identifying the work to be performed and whether the person is a union member. These contracts are especially important in Right to Work states, where union membership is required for employment.
- *Noncompetition agreements* forbid employees from working for a competitor. They should include adequate compensation.
- *Work schedules* clarify when an employee is working and when he is vacationing. Taking vacation time is often mandatory. While an employee is vacationing, his work functions are temporarily assumed by another worker, and an auditor may conduct a discovery audit to ensure that the employee has not engaged in any improper or illegal activities.
- *Confidentiality agreements* ensure that sensitive information is not disseminated outside the organization. Contractors and employees should sign confidentiality agreements; otherwise, the organization is exposed to substantial risk.
- *Ethics statements* clarify in precise detail the difference between ethical and unethical behavior. In most cases, any action that hurts the organization in exchange for personal gain is unethical.

INSURANCE

Insurance is a transference risk strategy that should complement other risk-reduction strategies. It transfers financial responsibility for an asset to a third party. Auditors should ensure that corporate assets have at least a minimum level of insurance protection and that the insurance is genuine; so-called *self-insurance* is not legitimate because the organization is assuming full financial liability for its assets. When obtaining insurance, an organization should compare the benefits of insurance against its actual cost.

RIGHT TO AUDIT

A right to audit obligates a third-party vendor or service provider to submit to an audit. Outsourcing contracts should include a right to audit; otherwise, many third-party contractors will likely decline a full audit and, instead, provide a copy of an SAS-70 form, which only includes the information that the contractor wants to provide, rather than the information that is necessary for a complete audit.

PERFORMANCE MANAGEMENT

Performance management measures the progress of a particular work activity against a set of unbiased performance metrics, and reports these findings to executive management and stakeholders. Metrics often rate the activity's level of compliance to IT controls, and are especially important in controlling IT budgets and noncompliant activities. Metrics represent an objective, quantitative assessment. For instance, a *KPI* or *key performance indicator* is normally calculated by averaging the historical performance of work activities. Despite their objective nature, metrics are often converted into non-numerical rankings, such as excellent, good, fair, and poor. Executives should create clear and open lines of communication for the reporting of performance metrics.

BUSINESS PROCESS REENGINEERING

Organizations will fail unless they change and redesign their existing business processes to incorporate new methods and technologies. Business process reengineering, or BPR, is a set of activities that facilitate change and redesign by analyzing current processes and rethinking business assumptions. Certain assumptions and their corresponding business rules may no longer be valid. Similarly, certain processes may have become inefficient or outmoded. BPR seeks to simultaneously increase productivity and reduce operating costs by focusing on three areas:

- *Improving techniques* – May involve incorporating new techniques or eliminating process steps that have become unnecessary in maintaining quality
- *Improving business efficiency* – Occurs as the process is repeated and workers increase their skill level; increased business efficiency means fewer quality inspections.
- *Incorporating new requirements* – Becomes necessary as laws and regulations change

BPR involves the following steps:

- *Envision:* Employees should envision a deficiency, and identify steps and activities to promote improvement. Then, they should seek sponsorship from the organization for their improvements.
- *Initiate:* The organization initiates a BPR by assigning a project team, establishing objectives, and creating and approving a BPR plan.
- *Diagnose:* The team should document, analyze, and understand current processes.
- *Redesign:* The team must create and document new processes that fulfill objectives.
- *Evaluate:* The team must monitor and analyze new processes to make certain they are performing as intended. Afterwards, continuous improvement processes can be implemented.

BPR Benchmarking

BPR teams often use benchmarking as a means of analyzing processes. Auditors can acquire benchmarks through published standards or self-assessment. Benchmark comparison involves the following steps:

- *Plan* – The BPR team must create a plan by determining the process that will be benchmarked and determining a system of measurements.
- *Research* – The team gathers baseline information for both the process and the comparison.
- *Observation* – The team collates data and compares it against the findings of a benchmark partner.
- *Analysis* – The team analyzes the data by applying specific tools and techniques.
- *Adaptation* – The team documents its findings as well as the impact of those findings on business goals.
- *Improvement* – The organization implements the new processes, monitors their output, and enacts continuous improvement procedures.

BPR Risks

The act of changing or altering processes always poses risks; therefore, the organization must identify possible risks before any BPR operations can commence. In doing so, it must consider three primary risk areas: design area risks, implementation area risks, and operational/rollout risks. *Design area risks* are posed by failures within the design process, often due to inadequate resources and developmental time. Repairing process design failures may require additional time and resources that the organization is unable to commit.

Design area risks include the following categories:

- *Sponsorship risks* – Include poor leadership, bad communication, and organizational executives who do not support the BPR operation
- *Scope risks* – Include poorly defined scopes, no access to protected processes, and projects that do not address an organization's strategic needs
- *Skill risks* – Include projects that are too inclusive to define accurately, and poor development of solutions and new ideas
- *Political risks* – Include organizational resistance to change and sabotage

BPR Implementation Area Risks

Implementation area risks are all the opportunities for failure during the lifetime of a BPR project. They can be classified under the following categories:

- *Scope risks* – Include poor scope definition, schedule variance, and high costs
- *Technical risks* – Include the limitations of an organization's information technology or software, difficulty of project, disagreements over terms and vocabularies, and implementation problems related to delay or excessive scope changes
- *Leadership risks* – Include management that does not support the BPR operation, fights over project ownership, constantly changes personnel, or fails to see a need for the project
- *Transition risks* – Include losing project staff and poor staff focus while implementing the project

Operation/Rollout Area Risks

Operation/rollout area risks are posed by various human, management, and technical factors. They can occur in spite of careful plan, and include the following categories:

- *Technical risks* – Include problems relating to software, insufficient testing, operational issues, inadequate support, and data integrity
- *Cultural/human risks* – Include persistent organizational resistance to proposed changes, ambiguous explanations of outcome, and insufficient training
- *Management risks* – Include persistent struggles over power and ownership, insufficient training and communication, and sabotage via passive and active means

A process should not be included in a BPR project unless it has a definite problem. Once a problem has been identified, project management should only reengineer the process if it would bring additional value to the organization. This value determination can be made using a *ROI, or return on investment,* calculation.

BPR Tools of Implementation

Organizations use the following tools to define and document processes that are being changed during BPR:

- *Benchmarking* is the process of evaluating the process being altered against a similar process.
- *Process maps* include diagrams and flow charts that help define the process.
- *Process controls* ensure the completion of every process step using checkpoints and checklists.
- *Roles and responsibilities* are assigned to identify the person or persons responsible for a particular process or activity. This information is then documented.

- *Tasks and activities* are assigned to define the person responsible for performing a specific work function, to explain the impact of the function on the overall project, and to document this information using a work breakdown structure (or WBS).
- *Data process restrictions* define all information and information sources available from and for the process.
- *Risk assessment* is the process of identifying sources of external and internal risk to the project.

BPR Basic Principles

When conducting BPR projects, the BPR team should adhere to a set of basic principles:

- Examine processes and determine if they can be simplified, consolidated, integrated into one process, automated, or removed.
- Facilitate permanence by creating parallel processes.
- Standardize operations by creating a uniform set of processes, tools, and procedures.
- Arrange processes in a logical order.
- Implement controls that provide the best and most efficient governance possible.
- Only enact change where it is needed.
- Empower staff members to decide operational issues.

Auditors of BPR projects must have specialized skills and/or knowledge in the following areas: CISA auditing standards; organizational procedures and processes; the specific area being audited; information systems auditing; interpersonal skills; and general management.

Categories for Processes

Auditors should ensure that BPR projects properly categorize each process being evaluated. Although each organization has its own specialized classification system, most processes fall under the following categories:

- *Working processes* use controls that fulfill IT audit specifications, and meet quality, budget, and business requirements. They are repeatable, measuring level two on the CCM.
- *Marginal processes* have one or more damaged components, such as efficiency, output, budget, quality, etc. They may fail audit reviews, and measure level one on the CCM. If they require redesign, BPR must determine if the redesign is adding value.
- *Nonworking processes* rank at the top of the BPR priority scale because certain components are not functioning.

- *Excluded processes* are exempted from inclusion in the BPR project. Exemption is only granted if specific criteria are present, such as impermanence, repeated and frequent use, being already scheduled for replacements, or having high value.

Auditors should also be able to evaluate processes using the value equation (ROI).

BPR Project Steps

First Step

Envisioning is the first step of a BPR project: the project manager seeks out and justifies a need for BPR, and then acquires sponsorship and formal approval for the project. Formal approval requires a project charter, which contains the following BPR project information:

- *Project title* – Names the project and provides a synopsis of BPR goals and objectives
- *Product description* – Lists the intended project deliverables
- *Project manager* – Identifies the project manager, explains his responsibilities and authority, and specifies if the project has a support committee
- *Business reason* – Explains rationale behind the BPR project and its expected benefits
- *Signature* – Normally authorizes the project

Second Step

Initiation is the second step of a BPR project: Project management creates a project plan, establishes project goals, and gets approval for the plan. The initiation step includes creating and identifying the following project elements:

- *Project scope* – Includes goals, objectives, milestones, and deliverables
- *Budget* – estimate of project costs, which are presented to management for approval
- *Project schedule* – Identification and distribution of project resources, and alignment of the time estimate of the project charter with the scope of work
- *Quality plan* – Identification of quality requirements as well as the processes for measuring and documenting those requirements
- *Project risks* – Used to create a risk register
- *Staffing plan* – Estimate of human resources, in which roles and responsibilities are assigned according to the WBS
- *Project communications plan* – Explains communication needs
- *Procurement plan* – Identifies which project resources must be procured from third parties

Third Step

Diagnosis is the third step of a BPR project: the BPR team determines which processes must be altered or reengineered, and then documents and analyzes these processes before any changes are made. Processes should not undergo any reengineering that does not bring additional value to the organization; therefore, the team should calculate a ROI (which indicates the expected value increase) for each suggested change. Without proof that BPR benefits the organization, executive management is not likely to approve it.

Fourth Step

Redesigning is the fourth step of a BPR project: processes are actually reengineered in accordance with project goals, and each reengineered process represents a measurable deliverable. Project management determines if new deliverables fulfill project goals and budgetary constraints by applying various performance measurements to the new processes. The team should also maintain constant communication with stakeholders, informing them of project progress.

Fifth Step

Reconstruction is the fifth step of a BPR project: the BPR team integrates the reengineered processes into the organization using change control. If change control is not carried out properly, the new processes will likely encounter significant resistance from organizational employees.

Sixth Step

Evaluation is the sixth and final step of a BPR project: the BPR team closes out the project, and documents any lessons learned or values received. Executive management must formally accept and approve the new processes before the project is officially completed. The new processes are monitored and reviewed as continuous improvement plans are implemented. The evaluation step occurs over a period of time set forth in the project charter.

Government Standards

The *National Institute of Standards and Technology (NIST)* is a federal agency that creates and sets standards for information technology. Although only government organizations must abide by these standards, NIST serves as a basis from which private companies and organizations have created practices and techniques. Standards for IS systems can also be found internationally. For instance, the *International Standards Organization (ISO)* incorporates a number of US security standards and British security standards into ISO standard 17799. British information security is regulated by *British Standard 7799-1.* Auditors should research and understand both American and international standards, because clients will use each of them as bases for implementing IS systems.

IS Acquisition, Development, Implementation, Operations, Maintenance, and Support

CAAT

Computer-assisted audit tools, or CAAT, assist the IS auditor in gathering data and performing calculations. Although these tools are capable of performing complex calculations and tests that are very difficult for humans, they are often cost-prohibitive and require intensive training. CAAT programs perform the following tasks: conducting compliance tests, substantive tests, and vulnerability tests; examining user logs to ensure password compliance; determining if the host system is vulnerable by analyzing the system configuration; evaluating particular software applications; examining network traffic and protocols; determining the number of software licenses; tracking software applications using mapping tools and test data; and, in some cases, composing actual reports based on the findings.

The following CAAT programs enable online auditing:

- *Online event monitoring* – Tracks various system and transaction logs, generates reports for the auditor, and alerts the auditor when certain events occur. Online event monitoring is a low-complexity tool, and includes intruder detection systems and virus scanners.
- *Snapshot audit* – Evaluates a transaction by examining it as a series of data elements (known as snapshots). These elements are arranged sequentially, and then studied by the auditor. Snapshot audits are a medium-complexity tool.
- *Embedded audit module (also known as EAM or integrated test facility)* – Generates a group of fake transactions and processes them with real transactions. In this way, the auditor can evaluate the performance of the fake transactions. EAM is a high-complexity tool.
- *Embedded program audit hooks* – Alert the auditor of problematic transactions so he can examine them before they become a major issue. This is a low-complexity tool.
- *Continuous and intermittent simulation, or CIS, audit* – Compares transactions against a set of criteria, and audits those transactions that meet the criteria. When the audit is complete, the CIS software seeks out a new transaction. CIS is a medium-complexity tool.
- *System control audit review filed with embedded audit modules, or SCARF/EAM* – Tracks embedded audit modules at the system-level. Though very effective, this program is rarely used due to its extensive programming requirements. SCARF/EAM is a high-complexity tool.

Sourcing

Every company must address the *sourcing* issue, which involves determining a location and a method for performing key work functions, such as manufacturing, customer support, accounting, payroll, printing, human resources, record management, and software development. These work functions can be performed either *on-site* or *off-site* by means of insourcing, outsourcing, or hybrid sourcing.

- When a company chooses *insourcing*, its own personnel will perform the work function.
- If the company chooses *outsourcing*, it contracts a third-party vendor to perform the work function. Outsourcing often involves finding cheaper labor at an *offshore* location, such as India, China, or Russia.
- Yet another method is *hybrid sourcing*, which combines characteristics of insourcing and outsourcing: companies maintain control over the work function while contracting any collateral work over to third-party vendors. This method is particularly useful when a company lacks the resources to take full advantage of an economic opportunity and must embark on a joint venture.

Sourcing Decision Considerations

A company's preference to insource, outsource, or hybrid source will be based on several different factors: the benefits of insourcing versus those of outsourcing; the competitive advantage provided by each type of sourcing; the location where the work will be performed; the benefits of going offshore; and, the disadvantages of bringing work back from an offshore location. Although companies are seeking skilled labor at low wages when they move off shore, they should also consider factors such as the taxation practices, exchange rates, legal restrictions, and cultural differences of other countries. These can undermine any advantage gained by cheap labor. For instance, when a company chooses to outsource, it increases turnaround and cycle time. It also may alienate its American clientele.

Operation

An operation is any procedure intended to create a predefined result. The goal of operations management is addressing user requests in a consistent and effective manner, and remedying the problems encountered during daily business operations. When evaluating operations management, IS auditors should ensure that operation managers and their staff are directly supporting the technical responses set forth by middle management. In turn, these technical responses should be supporting the strategic objectives created by executive management. Auditors must be able to differentiate between volume of work and effectiveness of work; even the busiest workers are of little help to the organization if their work is not supporting business objectives. Auditors should also ensure the organization is capable of sustaining its processes, which is only possible if three factors are present:

- Well-documented, written procedures
- Sufficient amount of staff
- Highly integrated staff, including good communication and clearly defined roles and responsibility for each staff member

ORGANIZATION CHART

An *organizational chart* is essential in defining roles and responsibilities. It lists each position and describes its corresponding job function within the organization. It also identifies the person in charge for every level, and explains the reporting relationships between positions. Auditors should ensure that an auditee's organizational chart is both current and accurate. Inaccurate or out-of-date charts reveal internal control problems. Most organizational charts include the following IT positions:

- *IT director* is an upper-management position responsible for managing the group, supervising IS/IT managers, giving orders to operations managers, and carrying out the plans of executive management.
- The *IT operations manager* supervises an IT staff, which operates in areas such as software development, network administration, information security, and help desk. IT operations managers handle user complaints, address problems, and ensure that solutions are created and implemented.
- *Systems architects* create new system designs and layouts by examining information collected by the system's analyst. The new system should help the organization generate revenue.
- *Systems analysts* collaborate with the system's end users to determine system requirements and to devise screen and report layouts. He then reports this information to the systems programmer and the application programmer. The systems analyst helps implements business methods in IT.
- *Systems programmers* write new software designed to implement some change in the operating system. Auditors should understand that the actual responsibilities of the systems programmer positions will vary depending on the organization. For instance, organizations that use MS Windows rely on the Microsoft Corporation for their programming needs. However, if an organization uses UNIX or a similar system, the system programmer rewrites the internal functions of the existing operating system.
- *Applications programmers* write software that assists end users by providing automated solutions.

- *Information security managers (or ISMs)* establish security policies for all information systems, and ensure that organizational procedures are following those policies. An ISM is actively involved in monitoring, accrediting, and certifying security systems. Auditors should ensure that the ISM is using the appropriate security metrics (e.g. NIST 800-53), and that the person fulfilling the ISM role has the proper training and certifications (e.g. ISACA Certified Information Security Manager, IISSCC Certified Information Systems Security Certification Consortium, etc.)
- *Change control managers* evaluate the staff's compliance with all applicable plans, controls, and procedures. This function can be performed by any number of persons, and is necessary to the quality assurance process.
- *Network administrators* facilitate and maintain data communication through the network. These individuals implement the Simple Network Management Protocol (SNMP) to monitor the devices through which information is transmitted. Network administrators also control IP addresses, assist system administration, and maintain network security devices, including firewalls, gateways, scanners, and detection systems.
- *Database administrators* maintain the database, preserving the information therein.
- *Server administrators* monitor server hardware and determine software settings. The actual responsibilities of the systems administrator depend entirely on the organization's operating systems. If the organization uses Microsoft systems, the server administrator merely chooses the software setting from a menu. However, if the organization uses UNIX, the administrator may create utilities by rewriting or altering software.
- *Data entry staff* is the people responsible for entering data. For large amounts of information, an organization may hire data entry professionals. However, in today's IT world, data entry is often performed by end users via the Internet; in this case, organizations should implement certain controls to maintain data integrity.
- The *help desk* is the first line of IT assistance for end users experiencing software or hardware problems. Help desk personnel abide by a set of policies and procedures designed to remedy basic problems. If the user has a more complex issue, help desk personnel will forward his problem to the appropriate senior IT staff. The help desk is usually manned by junior IT staff, whose performance is evaluated using a set of metrics.
- *Computer operator* is a junior-level position with the following responsibilities: helping the system and database administrators; starting software programs; stopping software programs; recording error and issue logs; reprioritizing jobs; seeking out potential problems; and taking complex problems to senior-level IT staff.

- *Media librarians* ensure all organizational data is properly and securely stored. The librarian is a junior-level position responsible for tracking information storage media (CDs, tapes, disks, portable memory devices, etc.), properly destroying media when necessary, and recalling media when required by an audit. The librarian tracks each storage medium using a *data set*, which explains the informational contents of the medium, where it is stored, and when it was created and last accessed. Backup media is normally stored offsite. Legal action may result if the librarian cannot account for media.

Compensating Controls

By clearly defining and separating IT roles, the organization ensures that every person is answerable to someone else, and that no one is capable of arbitrarily carrying out an action or taking assets. Organizational charts help define and maintain separation between IT roles; however, because they cannot account for every possible contingency, compensating controls are needed to remediate errors, mistakes, and fraudulence.

Compensating controls include the following activities:

- *Auditing* can occur internally (self-assessment) or externally (independently). Audit logs are of paramount importance in maintaining internal controls.
- *Job rotation* involves alternating personnel between different job functions on a cyclical basis. This lessens the possibility of fraudulence, and requires that employees be trained in multiple job functions.
- *Transaction logs* contain information that enables the organization to detect specific problems or issues if they are present. Auditors should ensure that the organization is reviewing logs regularly and thoroughly.
- *Reconciliation* involves auditing organizational records by comparing them against each other. Reconciliation looks to validate conclusions and guarantee consistency among records.
- *Exception reports* are sent to the supervisor when a worker discovers a computer processing error or an audit log omission. The supervisor analyzes the report and decides on a course of action that fulfills organizational policies and procedures.
- *Supervisor review* is the final compensating control. The supervisor evaluates the effectiveness of other compensating controls by observing their performance and conducting interviews.

Change Control

Change control includes processes for managing the implementation of change. It enables change to occur in an orderly and regulated manner, thereby minimizing confusion and resistance among organizational personnel. It also allows the organization to monitor and respond to any unexpected consequences brought about by the change, such as a drop in the effectiveness of existing processes and settings. In most organizations, internal auditors will be very active in the change control process; they will attend meetings, lend expertise, and determine if requested changes fulfill best practices and all applicable procedures. Auditors evaluate every level of organizational planning—strategic, long-term, and operational. Each level should be supported by the level beneath it, so that the daily operational tasks are helping to fulfill the overarching business objectives and strategic goals. Auditors make certain that the IT controls are maintaining this alignment.

Computer Component Groups

A computer's first component group includes three types of devices: CPU (Central Processing Unit), high-speed CPU memory cache, and RAM (Random Access Memory).

- The CPU is the central component in this group, and is supported by the other two. Using an arithmetic logic unit, it performs complex calculations far more quickly and accurately than any human can. The high-speed memory cache serves as a buffer between the CPU and RAM, and enables the CPU to operate at the highest possible speed and efficiency. RAM is solid-state memory, considerably slower than the other components but necessary to the CPU's efficient operation.
- The second component group includes data transmission channels, such as individual connectors and data buses. These input/output channels link the CPU with the high-speed memory cache and RAM.
- A computer's third component group consists of data storage devices, which include removable devices (such as jump drives) and fixed devices (such as internal data storage disks). Computers perform their startup activities, also known as initial program loads or IPLs, using fixed internal devices.

Time-Sharing

Time-sharing occurs when more than one person is using the same CPU. Although a single CPU can only process one request at a time, its processing speed should be fast enough that users do not experience any noticeable lag. Additional requests are stored in the memory until the CPU receives an interrupt command; then, it exchanges the current request for one stored in memory. Time-sharing can cause two serious problems for systems with only one processor:

- Certain programs, such as graphing software, can slow down the CPU due to their extensive processing requirements.
- Interrupt commands disrupt security programs, leaving the system vulnerable.

Multiprocessor Computers

Multiprocessor computers contain multiple CPUs. Through a technique known as *pipelining,* they alleviate the problems associated with time-sharing a single processor: A primary processor (designated CPU 1) stacks and allocates work tasks to other CPUs (designated CPU 2, CPU 3, etc.). CPU 1 performs no actual work tasks; instead, its sole responsibilities are checking input and output and distributing work to other processors. Multiprocessor computers are common in organizations with extensive processing requirements or high-level security needs. Multiple CPUs also have the ability to perform *interrupt masking*, which prevents important work actives from being interrupted.

STANDARD FUNCTIONS ON COMPUTERS

Any computer purchased commercially should perform the following tasks: interact with peripheral devices; run a common software program and operating system; store and retrieve data via a file system; manage communications and work allocation between the CPU and programs; regulate access to secure systems and information; and provide a *shell*, which is the graphical interface intended for users. Computers in an IT environment may fulfill the following functional roles:

- *User workstation* - Solves problems by using various applications and programs (e.g. Internet Explorer, Microsoft Excel)
- *Appliance or special-purpose device* - A computer that is specially built and configured to carry out dedicated processing (e.g. network routers, Web caches)
- *Database server* - Stores, arranges, and regulates access to information
- *File server* - Stores and allows shared access to files
- *Website server* - Stores and allows shared access to files
- *DNS server* - Seeks out IP addresses using domain names

PRIMARY COMPUTER CLASSES

Computers can be classified in four primary categories based on their size, processing power, and throughput, which indicate the amount of information they can process over a specific time interval. The categories are: mainframe computers, supercomputers, minicomputers, and microcomputers.

- *Mainframe computers* have tremendous processing power and throughput, and offer many advantages: multithreading capability, meaning they can carry out thousands of programs in unison; security features with multiple security levels, duty segregation, and internal control reporting; financial controls capable of reporting and charging users for access to the mainframe; virtual system capable of dividing resources; years of stable, continuous operation; and system support programs capable of lasting decades. Mainframe computers tend to be large, with the biggest ones occupying entire rooms. They are also very expensive, starting at $50,000 and peaking at prices well over $20 million.

- *Minicomputers (or midrange computers)* lack the processing power and throughput of a mainframe, but provide a cheaper alternative for organizations of limited size and financial means. Although midrange computers have security controls that are inferior to mainframes, they often have many of the same processing functions, especially if they run a UNIX operating system.
- *Microcomputers* include PCs, laptops, and most other systems designed to fulfill the requirements of an individual user—requirements that are often overlooked by a larger mainframe. Microcomputers can support multiple users if they have the proper operating system and hardware. Their most prominent drawbacks are porous security controls.
- *Supercomputers* possess extremely rapid processing speeds. They are highly specialized computers capable of performing complex scientific calculations and predictions. Supercomputers can be large or small, and are normally built for a specific task.

Supervisory and Problem State

Supervisory state and problem state are the two basic modes under which most computers operate. The *supervisory state* is reserved for supervisory users, also known as administrators, superusers, or root users. It removes security controls and allows the highest level of access to programs and processing requests. Without this unrestricted level of access, the supervisory user would be unable to perform his primary job tasks, which include managing change, configuring and maintaining the system, and performing administrative functions. Every other user must operate under the *problem state*, which activates all security controls and denies access to high-level programs and processing requests. In this highly regulated state, the computer's sole purpose is solving problems.

Disk and Tape Management Systems

Tape management systems and *disk management systems* help ensure that data is securely stored and controlled. They automate the process of tracking and labeling data files, enabling a user to quickly identify the contents, status, and location of every data storage device. Auditors will examine these systems in order to determine whether the data has sufficient security controls and storage area.

Data Storage Media

- *Magnetic tape* – More prevalent than any other long-term data storage media, existing in both reel and cartridge forms. Common types of tape include videocassettes, 3590 cartridges, and 8 mm DDS. Although tapes generally have very high storage capacities, they tend to be costly and cannot be accessed without specific hardware and software. If the hardware is malfunctioning, the tape could be irreparably damaged.
- *Magnetic hard disks* – Can store megabytes and terabytes of information; are the most prevalent online storage media. May be permanently contained within a closed disk drive, or be grouped in a storage array known as a RAID, or Redundant Array of Inexpensive Disks. There are several RAID levels:

- *RAID 0* – A number of small disks work as a single larger disk without fault tolerance. Operating Mode: Striping across multiple disks
- *RAID 1* – Two live copies of data are created, thereby halving available drive space. Operating Mode: Mirrored drives
- *RAID 2* – Data is distributed among several drives, and corrected via parity code. Operating Mode: Hamming code for correction error
- *RAID 5* – Two copies of data are created while using less storage space than RAID 1. Operating Mode: Distributed parity over all drives
- *RAID 7* – Data is transferred at an extremely fast rate. Operating Mode: Optimized asynchronous transfer
- *RAID 0+1* – Data is transferred at an extremely high rate by combining first two RAID levels. Operating Mode: Striped sets in mirror sets
- *Read-only memory, or ROM* – Contains data that has been permanently programmed on semiconductor chips by fusing microscopic, integrated circuits. These chips cannot be transferred, nor can they be upgraded unless they are removed and replaced. ROM provides solid-state storage that is both nonvolatile and incapable of being altered or erased; consequently, it provides excellent security, but may prove very limiting if constant upgrades are necessary. The greatest benefit of ROM is extremely quick loading time.
- *Flash memory* – Possesses the characteristics of ROM but can be reprogrammed. Although its high storage capacity is generally viewed as a benefit, it can become a security problem if the device is misplaced, which is common due to its small size. Flash devices are often bootable with minimal security controls.
- *Magnetic soft disks* – Small, removable, and portable devices such as floppy disks and Zip drives, in which a reprogrammable disk is contained in a hard, plastic casing. Disks can hold between 1 megabyte and multiple gigabytes of data.
- *Optical CD-ROMs* – Can store up to 700 megabytes of read-only data, and are created with hardware, such as CD burners. CD-ROMs are very portable and especially useful when archiving or backing up information. They are commonly used to record music with an audio storage limit of 80 minutes.
- *Optical CD-RWs* – Storage capacity and portability of a CD-ROM, with the added benefit of being reprogrammable. A person can simply erase and rewrite all of the information stored on the disk.
- *Optical DVDs* – All the characteristics of an optical CD, but possess a data storage capacity of multiple gigabytes.

Security Problems Associated with RAID

Every computer has a set of *physical input/output ports (I/O)*, which enable communication with other computers and storage devices. Unfortunately, a person can use these ports to bypass security controls and gain an unrestricted level of access to the system; therefore, organizations must implement *port controls.* These include *physical security controls*, which safeguard physical access to the ports, and *logical controls*, which are software programs designed to protect data transfers.

PCs are especially vulnerable because they have so many different ports: USB, RS-232, keyboard, expansion slots, disk channels, etc. Mainframes are vulnerable through their terminal, modem, and LAN ports. To ensure that the organization has implemented all necessary port controls, auditors must be aware of every port on each computer.

OSI AND TCP/IP

Open System Interconnect Model, or OSI, is a network training model that separates data communication into multiple networking layers. Each layer of the network has its own special role, and supports the layer above it. *Transmission Control Protocol/Internet Protocol, or TCP/IP,* is a networking protocol. Like the OSI model, TCP/IP stratifies the network into multiple layers:

OSI Layers	TCP/IP Layers
Layer 7: Application layer	Application
Layer 6: Presentation layer	
Layer 5: Session layer	
Layer 4: Transport layer	Transport
Layer 3: Network layer	Internet
Layer 2: Data-Link layer	Data-Link
Layer 1: Physical layer	Network

The application runs at the topmost layer. The data is further processed and broken down for transmission at each subsequent layer. Finally, at the bottommost layer, the data is completely broken down and distributed through the network to other systems.

LAYER 1

Layer 1, or the *physical layer*, identifies the wiring and voltages necessary to establish, sustain, and break off an electrical connection between multiple computers or systems. Essentially, this layer is a description of functional specifications.

LAYER 2

Layer 2, or the *data-link layer*, defines the hardware drivers required to create a connection between multiple computers. Hardware drivers have transmit/receive functions that enable data transmission between network cards and their MAC (Media Access Control) address. Each MAC address is completely unique, and allows the network interface to identify which data transmissions are intended for it and which ones are not within its broadcast domain. If this traffic load exceeds 45% with an Ethernet network, it may congest the network, resulting in *collision*, which upsets the data linkage.

LAYER 3

Layer 3, or the *network layer*, includes protocols that direct a data transmission along a specific path and to a specific destination using an *Internet Protocol* (*IP*) *address*. Each system on the network has a unique IP address, and multiple systems can be grouped together to form larger *IP subnetworks*, or *subnets*. When sending information to a specific location, a computer first determines the IP address of that location. Then, the computer combines the IP address with its own MAC address. A router uses the IP address to determine the data's precise location within a subnetwork and the best possible path for that data through the network. Using an Address Resolution Protocol (ARP), computers and routers can match the IP address with the appropriate MAC address. In some cases, routers and computers may need to run a Reverse Address Resolution Protocol (RARP), which matches the MAC address with the IP address.

- *Network routing* is the method by which routers direct traffic to the correct locations along the network. There are two methods of routing: static and dynamic.
- In *static routing*, the network administrator manually enters a TO-FROM map containing every IP address into the routing table of each router. Although static routing is very secure, it is impractical for networks with complex or unpredictable traffic.
- In *dynamic routing,* routers use special protocol algorithms (RIP, OSF, etc.) to monitor pathways and inform other routers when changes such as dead routes and new available paths occur.

A number of events can trigger a route change, as for instance the addition of new devices to the network, equipment failure, and poor network configuration. To lessen the chance that a single router will disrupt the network by transmitting a faulty change to every other router, the system should be configured so that only the changes of trusted routers are accepted. Most networks will probably incorporate both static and dynamic routing.

Layer 4

Layer 4, or the *transport layer*, includes protocols that encapsulate the data for transport along the network. TCP (Transmission Control Protocol) is one such protocol. It methodically breaks down the data transmission into manageable segments. Each segment contains a sequencing number, which enables the destination computer to reconstruct the message. TCP is known as a reliable transport method because it provides delivery confirmation to the computer that sent the data. Other transport protocols, such as UDP (User Datagram Protocol), are considered unreliable because they rely on a connectionless datagram that does not send delivery confirmation; consequently, the receiving computer must correct any errors. UDP is generally less expensive.

Layer 5

Layer 5, or the *session layer*, includes the protocols that initiate and manage communication sessions between systems on the network. Using these protocols (such as SQL net database and Network File System), the user's system will set up, govern, and terminate data transmissions to other systems.

Layer 6

Layer 6, or the *presentation layer*, receives and converts data into usable forms for other layers. It determines the format and structure that are required to use the data. Layer 6 protocols can receive data from Layer 5 and reformat it into a usable form for Layer 7 and receive data from Layer 7 and reformat it into a usable form for Layer 5.

Layer 7

Layer 7, or the *application layer*, actually executes programs. Layer 7 protocols include DNS (Domain Name Server), HTTP (Hypertext Transfer Protocol), or SNA Gateways. DNS supports Layer 3 by matching domain names and IP addresses, and SNA gateway reformats data structures for the mainframe. Layer 7 can run programs such as databases, automation software like Microsoft Office, printers, and web browsers.

Local Area Network

Local Area Networks, or LANs, are simply localized computer networks, usually covering a home, office, building, or other small geographical area. LANs allow multiple computers to exchange information and partake in certain services, such as email, file sharing, and printing. Data is transmitted through the network using one of the following methods:

- *Unicast* allows two (and only two) computers to communicate. This method creates minimal network congestion.
- *Multicast* allows one computer to communicate with a predetermined group of computers simultaneously. Networking is impossible without this method.
- *Broadcast* allows one computer to communicate with every computer on the network simultaneously.

LANs are constructed using software and various physical media devices, such as routers, cables, hubs, and switches. The quality of these devices determines the network's speed and reliability. Signal attenuation (or degradation) and network disruption occur when the distance between network devices surpasses their operational length.

Ethernet

An Ethernet is a type of network usually configured with a bus or star topology. It is most often used when network traffic consists of voice or data transmissions and all network media are confined to one location. Ethernets are contention-based systems; consequently, every network device must compete to use the same cable. Because of this contention, the network is often subjected to *collisions*, which occur when multiple computers simultaneously transmit data and the transmissions collide with each other. *Collision domains* are formed where two or more computers are linked to the same media device. If they attempt to access the media simultaneously, a collision will occur. Ethernets use mechanisms designed to handle collisions and preserve transmission integrity. Ethernets may also have *broadcast domains,* which are groups of network devices that transmit to each other.

The Ethernet Mechanisms for Handling Collisions

Because collisions are so common, Ethernets have two primary mechanisms designed to preserve data integrity: CSMA/CD and CSMA/CA. *CSMA/CD* enables network devices to detect collisions and then retransmit their data. Upon detecting a collision, a device will cease transmitting its current message and alert all other network devices of that collision. At this point, all devices activate a random collision back-off timer, ceasing their transmissions. This enables the first device to resend its original message without degradation. The second method is *CSMA/CA,* which is a more preventive measure. A device alerts the entire network of its intention to send a transmission; as a result, all other network devices refrain from transmitting data until the threat of collision has passed.

Topology

Network Topology

Network topology describes the configuration of all network components, including its computers, cables, routers, hubs, switches, and other devices. Most networks will follow one of three standard topologies: bus, star, or ring. IS auditors should ensure that networks have the following controls:

- Redundancy and disaster plans, which prevent the failure of single device from disrupting the entire network for a long period of time.
- Configuration management plans, which explain network functions and performance monitoring.
- Proper network segmentation, which reduces collisions.
- Sufficient bandwidth, which enables network access.

Bus Topology

A bus topology connects the entire network using a single coaxial cable, which is wired through a connector port on every computer. Using *repeaters*, the IT department can boost data transmission through the cable, thereby expanding the network. Although bus topology is less expensive than other methods, it tends to become unwieldy if the network grows too large. Also, if the cable ever becomes severed, the entire network is disrupted.

Star Topology

A star topology connects every network node (computer workstations and other devices) to a central hub or switch. These hubs/switches should possess the necessary throughput to allow communication between all network nodes, and they should be properly *meshed* so that failure of one hub does not disrupt the entire network. Star topologies are the most common network design for the following reasons:

- Workstations can be placed virtually anywhere.
- Nodes can be added and replaced with minimal disruption.
- They provide cable redundancy, meaning that a failure of one station does not interrupt the entire network.

Because of the excess cable, star topologies tend to be expensive.

Using routers, the IT department can link multiple LANs without merging them into a single subnetwork. Before the invention of routers, two subnetworks could only be linked if they were combined into a single subnetwork, often creating traffic congestion. Routers can transmit a single signal from LAN 1 to LAN 2 without exposing LAN 2 to all the traffic of LAN 1, greatly reducing the chance of collision.

Ring Topology

A ring topology links all network devices in a closed loop, creating high speed and high performance. Because there is no hub or switch linking the network nodes (computer workstations and other devices), they rely on each other for communication; consequently, in a simple ring topology, a single malfunctioning device can disrupt the entire network. One type of ring topology that compensates for this shortcoming is the *IBM Token Ring,* which relies on dual concentric rings: A group of computers is linked to a *MAU*, or *media access unit.* The Token Ring consists of several MAUs, each of which is linked to an upstream MAU and a downstream MAU. This alignment allows data to be transmitted in multiple directions (upstream and downstream), enabling the network to avoid any break.

Network Meshing

Meshing increases redundancy by creating additional connections between critical *backbone* points on a network. Meshing is very common in star topologies; the IT department identifies all links across the network, and determines which alternate link should be used when the primary one is severed. This information is then entered into the router. Networks can be meshed using two primary methods:

- *Full mesh* – All critical backbone points have alternate links. This method is also known as N–1, where N is the total number of critical backbone points and N–1 is the complete amount of additional links.
- *Partial mesh* – Only some of the critical backbone points have alternate links. Organizations use this method when they cannot afford a full mesh.

Cable Plant

A cable plant is simply another name for a network cable installation. Although auditing does not require the ability to design a network, auditors should have a basic understanding of the three different cable types—UTP, coaxial, and fiber-optic—and their respective strengths and weaknesses.

- *Unshielded twisted-pair cable, or UTP,* is found frequently in star topologies and 10/100 M Ethernets, and is the most commonly used cable type due to its inexpensiveness. Its range is normally limited to 200 feet, but certain kinds of UTP can be extended up to 100 meters. UTP includes the following categories:
    - *CAT-3* or *category 3* (voice only)
    - *CAT-5* or *category 5* (data and voice)
    - *CAT-5e* or *category 5 enhanced* (data transmissions of 1 GB and 100 MHz)
    - *CAT-6* and *CAT-7* (highly rated but less common)

According to fire and safety regulations, UTP must use two types of jackets, including a plenum grade Teflon. UTP must remain twisted to prevent electrical interference.

- *Coaxial cable* contains a mesh shielding that protects it from electrical interference. It is an older form of cable used in earlier bus topology Ethernets, and has largely been replaced by faster cables, such as UTP. However, coax is still used in outdoor locations, locations where electrical interference is prevalent, and locations covering long distances (185 meters). A repeater can extend this range.
- *Fiber-optic cables* convey information by means of laser beams refracting off tiny glass fibers. Through a process known as *dense wave multiplexing*, a single cable is capable of carrying numerous data streams if each stream is a different wavelength (i.e. color). In fact, 12, 24, or 64 lasers can use a single cable. Fiber-optic cables have the advantages of high speed (between 1GB and 1,000GB) and unlimited bandwidth. However, they tend to be expensive and highly breakable due to their glass fibers. Common applications of fiber-optics include long-haul installations and backbone connections.

Network Components

The following network components:

- *Wi-Fi transmitters* are short-range, wireless communications devices. They link laptops, PDAs, and other handheld devices to the network. Although Wi-Fi communications are relegated to a very small area, they still require security. Wi-Fi transmitters are included in layer 1 of the OSI model.
- *Repeaters* extend a network's range by boosting electrical signals. In effect, repeaters receive data transmissions and repeat them to the next device, thereby overcoming long distances that would normally cause signal degradation. They are included in layer 1 of the OSI model.

- *Bridges* link two different networks by combining them into a single subnet. Depending on their configuration, they can either broadcast all data traffic across the subnet or filter traffic. Bridges are included in layer 2 of the OSI model.
- A *hub* links a group of network devices. It amplifies, sends, and retimes the electrical signals of each device across all access ports. In this way, data traffic is spread over the entire network. Hubs are included in layer 2 of the OSI model.
- A *switch* has all the capabilities of a hub, as well as a processor that can execute logic programs. Using this processor, a switch can selectively shunt out data traffic and establish a communication line between two ports, similar to a private line. Switches are included in layer 2 of the OSI model.
- A *router* can link two subnetworks without merging them into a single network. It can send an individual data transmission from LAN 1 to LAN 2 without exposing LAN 2 to all data traffic from LAN 1.

Virtual LANs, or VLANs

The following terms:

- A *virtual LAN, or VLAN,* simulates a subnetwork for a group of computers. It is created using the following techniques:
- A *port-based VLAN* is established at layer 1 of the OSI model, and is used for small networks, uplinks, and immobile systems. The IT department identifies which computers must be part of the virtual subnetwork, and manually links their access ports into the VLAN.
- A *MAC-based VLAN* is established at layer 2 of the OSI model. It identifies the proper MAC addresses, links them into the VLAN, and reconfigures the ports.
- A *policy/rule-based VLAN* is established at layer 3 of the OSI with support from layer 2. An advanced network switch examines network traffic, identifies the appropriate IP addresses, and implements an administrative rule to form a VLAN. This kind of VLAN can be implemented without workstation software, and can reconfigure without manual help if moved elsewhere.

DNS and DHCP

Domain Name Service, or DNS, enables a user to access a website even if he does not know its IP address. He simply types in a *fully qualified domain name*, or *FQDN*, and the router directs him to the appropriate location from its table of IP addresses. If a network administrator is using a DNS, he can change the IP address of a particular site without needing to alert anyone; he simply updates the DNS server to change the IP address while keeping the same FQDN.

Dynamic Host Configuration Protocol, or DHCP, automatically updates the DNS settings on a computer and configures the IP addresses and subnetwork masks. DHCP is carried out at layer 2 of the OSI model. Consequently, a computer can only make a DHCP request if it is on the same subnetwork as the DHCP; otherwise, the router will block out the request. The network administrator can overcome this problem by reconfiguring the router to its *DCHP-helper-address* setting. The Dynamic Host Configuration Protocol, or DHCP, involves the following steps:

1. The network administrator configures one computer on the network to be the DHCP server. He then enters a group of IP addresses into the server.
2. The DHCP server seeks out any IP packet header containing a type 67 code.
3. If a computer lacks an IP address as it is being booted, it will send out a type 67 request (which includes its MAC address) to the DHCP server. A type 67 code is a request for an IP address assignment.
4. The computer that sent the type 67 code waits.
5. When the DHCP server receives the type 67 request, it replies to the appropriate MAC address with a type 68 code.

The requesting computer accepts the type 68 code (provided it was received in time). The requesting computer then accepts the IP address, automatically reconfigures its settings, completes the boot up process, and starts communicating on the network.

WAN

A *Wide Area Network, or WAN*, is simply a computer network capable of covering a much wider geographical region than a LAN. Organizations implement WAN equipment and protocols at OSI layers 1, 2, and 3 (physical, data link, and network), and may rent communication lines from the telecommunications industry, creating networks that span multiple states. Public Switched Telephone Networks (PSTN) and Integrated Services Digital Network (ISDN) can provide dialup services for WANs, which can also utilize message switching, circuit switching, and packet switching. WANs communicate using three possible methods: *simplex*, meaning one direction; *half-duplex*, meaning one direction at a time; and, *full duplex*, meaning both directions simultaneously using separate circuits. WANs use both switch and dedicated circuits, and follow the same communication protocols that LANs follow.

Dialup Network Devices

A LAN can acquire access to a WAN using the following dialup devices:

- *Modem* – Accesses a WAN through a low-speed dial-up connection, and can be attached to either a router or an individual computer; modems are the least secure method for accessing WANs
- *Network access server* – Normally used with a modem pool
- *Router with LAN port* – Uses telephone circuits to create a connection
- *Channel service unit (CSU)* – Uses high-speed telephone circuits rather than a regular modem to establish connection at transmission speeds ranging from 1 MB to 44MB
- *Multiplexor* – Merges several low-speed dial-up connections into a single fast connection, or divides a single high-speed connection into several low-speed connections

Auditors ensure that all devices have the necessary monitoring and security controls. Organizations should create separation of duties by dividing each remote connection into its own subnetwork.

Wired Network Devices

Users can access a network using the following wired connections:

- *Asynchronous Transfer Mode (ATM)* – Transmits data cells along multiple paths (as many as 132) to the target destination, which will use the first cell that arrives and dispose of the rest. By relying on multiple paths as well as multiplexing and cell switching, this method greatly improves the likelihood of the data cell being delivered. Because of its reliability and quick transmission speed (155Mbps to 1GBps), ATM is one of the most popular connections.
- *Digital Subscriber Line (DSL)* – An inexpensive circuit that uses a standard telephone line, and transmits at a high frequency and relatively fast speed (368Kbps to 1.544Mbps). The high frequency of DSL prevents it from interfering with voice transmissions over the same line. This method is limited by range, and is only available in high-density regions.
- *Plain Old Telephone Service (POTS)* – Transmits data via a standard telephone line at the slow rate of 56 Kbs, and uses one half of the ISDN circuit. POTS is the only method that can be turned off when not in use. All other methods are considered to be constantly transmitting.
- *Integrated Services Digital Network (ISDN)* – Serves as the basis for the POTS method but can transmit at speeds as high as 1.54Mbps. It can send data, voice, and video, and is the most common medium for video conferencing. ISDN offers bandwidth at 128K and higher. Users can divide the 128K into two 56K connections.
- *International Telecommunications Standard X.25 (X.25)* – An older digital packet-switching protocol that is rarely used in current times but still serves as a reference model. It uses the *facility code*, which allows a user to determine a quality of service by changing various parameters in a field.
- *Frame-relay* – A type of packet-switching system that transmits at speeds between 1.544 Mbps and 22.4 Mbps. It is inexpensive, but tends to send data packets non-sequentially. Consequently, the target computers must have software capable of catching and resembling the packets. Non-sequential data transmission only poses problems for video.

Wireless Network Devices

Users can access a network using the following wireless connections:

- *Wi-Fi radio* has a maximum range of 1,500 feet, and relies on a transmitter/receiver that circumvents private radio channels using a digital spread spectrum (implemented at OSI layer 1). It often uses a cellular service. Wi-Fi is the most popular wireless connection, and is often found in fleet operations for the military and private industry.

- *Satellite radio* transmits data using a low-orbit satellite, which provides a massive service area. This method has a few notable drawbacks: it is expensive, relatively slow (between 9.6Bps and 4MBps), requires additional hardware, and has a 2 to 5 second lag time. However, it is the second most popular wireless connection and is often used in shipping and retail chains. Satellite uplinks can send video, data, fax, and telephone signals. Emergency response teams often use satellite phones.
- *Microwaves* transmit at speeds between 1MBps and 100MBps, and at distances from 1 to 30 miles. Microwaves are most effective with a direct line of sight and clear weather conditions, and are best suited for communications over cities and mountain ranges. Although microwave transmitters tend to have high construction and maintenance costs, they do not incur costs for repeated transmissions.
- *Lasers* are very similar to microwaves, transmitting at speed between 1MBps and 100MBps. Lasers also require a direct line of sight, and become disrupted by adverse weather conditions. They are often used to link multiple offices across a city.

Network Types

The following types of networks:

- *Metropolitan area networks (MANs)* link computers located in different buildings within the same city. They are larger than a LAN and smaller than a WAN.
- *Campus area networks (CANs)* link computers across different buildings within the same campus. They normally rely on fiber optics, cables, and other kinds of wireless transmitter.
- *Storage area networks (SANs)* use Ethernets, ATMs, or fiber optics to connect various types of file storage within a server farm.
- *Personal are networks (PANs)* connect handheld devices, such as PDAs, with a personal computer. The range of a PAN is normally limited to 10 feet or less.

RFID Tags

A radio frequency identification (RFID) tag is a short-range wireless communication device that consists of silicon chips and antennas. It enables automated tracking of products and inventory. IS auditors should be aware of the basic kinds of RFID tags. Passive tags, for instance, are detected by scanners at a certain distance, and are frequently used to track inventory. Some passive tags are small enough to be constructed into products or implanted into living hosts. Despite the privacy issues raised by such devices, hospitals have considered using them to track newborn children and elderly patients. Other, non-passive RFID devices may have the ability to broadcast signals. These tags receive queries from a broadcast source and then transmit a response using an imbedded transponder. Non-passive RFID devices are popular with law-enforcement agencies, which use them to gather surveillance information.

Network Management Tools

The syslog and automated cable tester are tools of network management, and assist the network administrator as he monitors network performance and identifies possible security breaches. A *syslog* monitors and records each instance in which a person logs into the system, and alerts the administrator of possible security violations. It transmits login messages to a centralized server, which aggregates the messages and the security alerts for auditing purposes. Syslogs can be implemented easily and require a minimal level of system resources. Their primary disadvantage is an inability to authenticate messages and preserve message integrity. A handheld *automated cable tester* ensures that network cables comply with all necessary certifications, including length, electrical, and signal requirements. Cable deficiencies account for 97% of all network troubles. Cables are certified and put into production if they pass all tests.

SNMP

Using a simple network management protocol (SNMP), a network administrator monitors and checks the status of routers, servers, gateways, hubs, and other network devices. Specifically, an SNMP performs the following tasks: monitors network devices and alerts the administrator of network problems; reboots and/or deactivates network devices; and changes system parameters. Each device under SNMP control should have a unique password; otherwise, it is automatically given one of the default passwords: *public* or *private*, which are known as *community strings*. Using these simple passwords, anyone can gain access to a network device if he knows the correct IP address. IS auditors should ensure that network administrators are creating and assigning unique passwords. Without unique passwords, SNMP is a weak security device.

Protocol Analyzer and RMON2

A *protocol analyzer*, also known as a *packet sniffer*, is another software tool that assists network administrators as they monitor and manage a network. It records all data transmissions and communications passing through a specific segment of the network, including the passwords used to gain access. A packet sniffer helps identify potential problems, but cannot see beyond the individual segment it is monitoring. Because sniffers capture passwords and user IDs, they can become major security risks if accessed by a hacker. The *remote monitoring protocol version 2, or RMON2,* can monitor every layer of the OSI network model simultaneously, recording hours or even years of transmissions and communication. This information is usually stored long-term within an SQL database. By contrast, a pocket sniffer can only monitor the first three layers of the OSI network model for a time period exceeding no more than several hours.

Strategic and Traditional Systems

Strategic systems enable an organization to drastically alter the manner in which its business is run, improve its business performance, and increase its competitiveness on the open market. Any improvement should be quantifiable through performance metrics. The goal of a strategic system is increasing the overall return on an investment by 10 times or more. *Traditional systems* assist organizational departments and employees as they carry out their functions. Although the goal of any organizational software is increasing profit while reducing operating expenses, traditional systems have far more modest goals than strategic systems in terms of augmenting investment return. Both strategic and traditional systems consist of software that has been uniquely designed and written for a specific organization. Organizations can ensure high quality in their software by following one of two models during software development: *capacity maturity model* (*CMM*) or *international standard model.*

ISO

International Organization for Standardization, also known as *ISO*, incorporates and promotes many American best practices for quality in manufacturing. Following the teachings of Joseph Juran, Philip Crosby, and W. Edwards Deming, ISO seeks to reduce the number of product defects in all processes. Software development usually follows one of three possible ISO standards: ISO 15504, ISO 9001, and ISO 9126.

- *ISO 15504, or Spice*, is simply a variation on CMM. It rates processes according to five levels:
    - ISO Level 0: Incomplete – Process is missing.
    - *ISO Level 1: Performed* – Process has been carried out successfully.
    - *ISO Level 2: Managed* – Process is managed.
    - *ISO Level 3: Established* – Process is established.
    - *ISO Level 4: Predictable* – Process generates a consistent output.
    - *ISO Level 5: Optimized* – Process can be continuously improved.
- According to *ISO standard 9001:2000* (which was updated in the year 2000), an organization cannot claim ISO compliance unless it writes and documents a comprehensive quality management manual, which must include processes for the following: training organizational employees; increasing the competencies of employees; and evaluating and selecting vendors. Auditors should ensure that such a manual exists and that its processes are being implemented.
- Organizations seeking ISO compliance should also incorporate *ISO standard 9126-2:2003*, which details the metrics by which software products and quality should be assessed. These metrics evaluate software quality against six criteria:
    - Reliable and consistent output
    - Software functionality
    - Efficient use of resources
    - Ease of transference between different environments
    - Modifiable while retaining present performance
    - User-friendliness

Although ISO compliance does not ensure better software quality, it does improve an organization's standing amongst investors and increases the likelihood of creating a good product.

Software Decision-Making

The IT steering committee must select and design software that best supports and aligns with the organization's strategic objectives. When making a software decision, the committee normally relies on two methods: critical success factor and scenario approach. *Critical success factors, or CSFs,* are the informational needs of an organization as determined by each manager. CSFs are influenced by a variety of factors: internal organizational issues; external issues such as competition and the state of the economy; and issues that are specific to a certain industry or market. In the *scenario approach*, the committee creates a group of hypothetical scenarios based on current organizational trends, assumptions, and events. The committee then selects the scenario that is most likely to occur, and uses it for a planning exercise. The purpose of the exercise is identifying new strategic objectives, CSFs, and business assumptions that are no longer valid.

Business Justification

An organization will not undertake a project unless it produces a quantifiable financial benefit. This benefit is known as a *business justification*. Before any project can commence, the organization must prove a justification by undertaking the following steps:

- *Establishing a business need* – A need can be external or internal to the organization. External needs can come about because of law changes, increased competition in the marketplace, etc. Internal needs are usually revealed by performance metrics or the IT steering committee.
- *Identifying work effort* – Project personnel write a project plan and create a process flowchart that details CSFs. This step also determines the parties who will perform the actual project work.
- *Summarizing project impact* – The business impact is shown through both quantitative and qualitative techniques.
- *Presenting benefits* – Management must be shown reasons why the project is necessary. These reasons may include increasing profit and productivity, correcting a problem, or improving customer relations.

The following terms related to software decisions and the IT steering committee:

- *Alignment* – Organizational software supports objectives.
- *Impact* – The manner in which new software enhances work methods and cost efficiency.

- *A buy vs. build decision* – Determines purchasing decisions regarding commercial vs. design custom software. When making this decision, the committee will hold brainstorming sessions and consider the following points:
    - Software's impact on business objectives
    - Evidence and metrics showing that the software will actually support (align with) business objectives
    - Whether or not the organization is actually capable of creating custom software
    - The amount of customization necessary in the software
    - Availability of commercial software that meets business requirements
    - Internal controls required to safely and securely operate software
    - Time constraints determining when software must be implemented
    - Means of acquiring funding for the software
    - Types of controls required to execute transactions in an accurate, secure, and timely manner

Request for Proposal (RFP)

A request for proposal, or RFP, becomes necessary when an organization is required to design and write custom software. The organization appoints a project team, who distributes RFPs to a select number of third-party vendors, asking them to submit a bid or proposal for creating the software. An RFP usually includes the following information: a cover letter detailing the purpose of the RFP and directions for responding; synopsis of the organization's history; criteria for reviewing and selecting a bid; thorough explanation of software requirements; inquiries concerning the vendor's history, existing clientele, and areas of expertise and training; request for demonstrations and visits to the auditor's place of business; and a request for an estimate on desired work. After the vendors respond, the project team must review each proposal and select the one that best fits its selection criteria, which are often shaped by ISO standards 9001 and 9126-2. Auditors ensure that the selection process is both fair and objective.

Selecting a Vendor Proposal

The process of selecting a vendor proposal should be as fair and unbiased as possible; for this reason, auditors ensure that each proposal is weighed against the following criteria:

- Time and resource estimates
- Extent to which a proposal gives a competitive advantage within the marketplace
- Conformance to organizational business requirements
- Modifications necessary to fulfill project requirements
- Expected financial benefits to the organization versus the cost of the proposed system (including the method for calculating those benefits)
- Financial stability of the vendor
- Evidence that the vendor has performed a risk analysis

- Software escrow rights if the vendor goes out of business
- Support (e.g. upgrades, telephone and emergency assistance, maintenance, and training) provided by the vendor

Auditors should be wary of proposals that do not address these issues, as well as of vendors who provide excessively low estimates. After being awarded the project, these vendors often overcharge on a series of expensive change orders.

Managing Software Development

Auditors should understand the two primary organizational philosophies in software development: evolutionary and revolutionary. According to the *evolutionary* viewpoint (the more conservative philosophy), programming errors are usually the results of poor project planning; therefore, the most important work is performed during the planning and design phases. During evolutionary development, software is often distributed incrementally, with each additional increment increasing the functionality and features of the previous edition. The *revolutionary* approach relies on fourth generation programming languages, or *4GL*, which eliminates the need for a trained programmer in software development. Users can create software based on their individual needs by simply experimenting with the language. The revolutionary philosophy gives business users full control over the project's outcome; unfortunately, it also poses great risk due to an absence of internal controls and well-defined objectives.

SDLC Phases

According to ISACA, the lifecycle of every software program follows six phases. This lifecycle is known as the System Development Life Cycle, or SDLC, and consists of the following phases:

- *Phase 1 (Feasibility Study)* – Project management identifies the financial and operational benefits of the proposed software system.
- *Phase 2 (Requirements Definition)* – IT steering committee determines and defines a need for the new system.
- *Phase 3 (System Design/Selection)* – Organization chooses one of the following options:
    - *Build/design* a custom software program.
    - *Buy/select* a commercial software program.
- *Phase 4 (Development/Configuration)* – Organization chooses one of the following options based on its decision in Phase 3:
    - *Develop* (write and test) the custom software program.
    - *Configure* settings of commercial program.
- *Phase 5 (Implementation)* – Project team installs the software, and gets the proper accreditation and certification for the system.

Phase 1

Phase 1, or the *feasibility study phase*, involves determining and thoroughly documenting a business need for new software. Project management identifies any strategic benefits, and justifies the proposed software based on cost, resource, and time estimates, as well as traditional project management techniques. Cost estimates are normally calculated using the *constructive cost model.* In phase 1, auditors consider the following questions:

- The business need for the new software according to the needs analysis documentation?
- Could an existing piece of software fulfill the business need? The risk mitigation strategy?
- Is acquiring new software a good decision based on the business needs and cost justifications?
- Does the project obtain management approval before moving to the second phase?

Management gives approval at a review meeting, which is held at the end of every phase and includes the executive chairperson, project sponsor, project manager, and other important personnel. The chairperson reviews project results, and approves or rejects the project.

Constructive Cost Model

The constructive cost model, or COCOMO, estimates the cost, schedule, and resource requirements of acquiring new software. It was created by Barry Boehm in 1981, and has since been supplanted by COCOMO II. *COCOMO II* can forecast the impact of cost, scheduling, and resource changes on software development. Both constructive cost models rely on the following estimation methods: source lines of code and function point analysis. *Source lines of code*, or *SLOC*, calculates estimates by counting each line of program code. *Function point analysis*, or *FPA*, categorizes each element of a software program according to the following functions:

- External input (comes from users and external applications)
- External output (sent to users, external applications, and reports)
- External inquiries (come from users and external applications)
- Internal files (store data inside the system database)
- External interfaces (determine the procedures for and location of accessing data)
- COCOMO II can also use the application composition, early design, or post-architecture submodels.

Phase 2

Phase 2, or the *requirements definition phase*, identifies and documents a list of specific business requirements for the proposed software. This list includes the inputs and outputs of the program, as well as the conditions and environments within which the program will be used. Business requirements can be identified using the ERD (entity-relationship diagram) technique, which also creates flowcharts that will be used in phase 3. Auditors evaluate the validity of these requirements by conducting interviews with organizational employees and examining project documentation, specifically the ERD and various flowcharts. Auditors also ensure the project has received management approval at a review meeting before moving on to phase 3. Approval is only given if all business requirements (including schedule forecasts) have been thoroughly defined, and the eventual users of the software have provided their own feedback and commentary.

ERD

The *entity-relationship diagram technique, or ERD,* is used during phase 2 of the SDLC. It helps identify and define software requirements by determining the relationships between entities. An entity is simply a database containing various data storage mediums (reports, memos, disks, etc.) relevant to the software project. A relationship may involve information, concepts, and personnel. An ERD first identifies information that will be used by the software. Then, it creates a *data dictionary*, which includes reference terms for each database element. Using this dictionary, it structures all information contained in the database within a *database schema*. With this information, the project team can create *high-level flowcharts*, which illustrate business logic, and *low-level flowcharts*, which display the transformation of data in a useful form at various steps of the process.

PHASE 3

Phase 3, or *the system design phase,* develops the work breakdown structure for the project as well as the basic plan and design for the software prototype, which will be written in phase 4. Any plan should create a separation of duties by implementing preventive controls, detective controls, and corrective controls. During phase 3, the project team decompiles flowcharts into separate program modules, and may use techniques such as reverse engineering, reengineering, and software baseline. Auditors at this phase should perform the following tasks:

- Reexamine flowcharts and software baseline.
- Ensure the software integrates all necessary controls and plans.
- Ensure the software design incorporates user feedback (gathered in phase 2) in the form of special features, screen and report layouts, etc.
- Confirm the software has received formal management approval at a review meeting before moving to the next phase.

At the review meeting, management examines the proposed design of the new software, its design features, risk analysis, cost estimates, and business assumptions.

PHASE 4

During phase 4, or the *development phase*, the software is written (*coded*), tested, and debugged. Programmers may use a number of programming languages (such as BASIC, Java, COBOL, etc.), depending on organizational preference, and are supported by systems analysts, who provide ideas and insight. At this phase, an auditor has the following responsibilities:

- Ensuring that a quality control process has been implemented on the software.
- Verifying that the program has been tested and debugged.
- Examining test results to ensure the software is reliable and complies with organizational objectives.
- Verifying the effectiveness of internal controls and safeguards within the software.
- Confirming the software has received formal management approval at a review meeting before moving to the next phase.

The review meeting examines test results and determines whether the software's actual performance coincides with expected results as set forth in the initial project objectives, design specifications, etc.

Quality Control in Software Development

Programmers must implement quality control standards and maintain a high-level of structure as they write code; otherwise, making modifications to the software is very difficult. Software coding that lacks structure is known as *spaghetti bowl programming.* Most programmers maintain high levels of structure by following a *top-down structure programming* model, which separates the program into individual modules. Each module carries out a specific task, and can be assigned to a different programmer. When all programmers have completed their work, the modules are assembled to create the finished program. The project team can easily remove and/or update individual modules.

Management ensures that the software project follows a planned schedule as closely as possible. The schedule should allow for some variance in cost and time estimates, and should track these variances using a *version control* system. Large variances may necessitate a *management oversight review* if they alter project requirements, methodology, or assumptions.

Programming Languages

Programming languages have become increasingly user-friendly with each subsequent generation. First-generation programming language (known as *machine language*) and second-generation programming language (known as *assembly language*) were very difficult to use, but were industry standards in the 1950s. Third-generation programming language came about in the 1960s, and was the first to incorporate clear English commands such as GOTO and THEN. It includes languages such as BASIC, C programming, and COBOL. Fourth-generation programming language (*4GL*) is the current industry standard. It allows users to write certain kinds of programs even if they are untrained in software development. However, these programs will only be capable of formatting reports and data files; a skilled programmer is still necessary to create the business logic and procedures that convert the information into a usable form. Fifth-generation programming languages have artificial intelligence that can learn using *fuzzy logic* and *neural weighing systems.*

IDE

Integrated development environment, or IDE, is a type of fourth-generation programming tool. It creates an environment within which software can be designed, coded, and debugged. IDE is important because most modern-day programmers do not write code manually; they devise the high-level business logic and allow the program (i.e. fourth generation programming language) to write the software. A popular, commercial type of IDE is the computer-aided software engineering tool, or CASE. Auditors should understand that phases 2, 3, and 4 of the SDLC are supported by the following CASE tools:

- Upper CASE supports SDLC phase 2. It helps to document and define business requirements, and to create an ERD with flowcharts.
- Middle CASE supports SDLC phase 3. It supports programmers as they create a basic plan for the software, including its data objects, structure, layout formats, and logical process flows.
- Lower CASE supports SDLC phase 4 by writing the actual program code.

Agile Development Method and RAD

The agile development method and rapid application development method (RAD) are fourth-generation programming techniques that are capable of speeding up software development. By implementing time-box management, the agile development method can generate numerous revisions of a prototype in a small period of time. Agile forces the programmer to code from memory; therefore, it is best suited for small groups of highly skilled and knowledgeable programmers. Because agile requires very little preplanning, its primary disadvantage is a lack of baseline requirement management. The rapid application development method, or RAD, relies on fourth-generation programming languages that are capable of carrying out substantial parts of the SDLC with little or no help from a programmer. RAD performs analysis at all SDLC phases except phase 1 – a major drawback, because phase 1 is very important to major business software applications. Both agile and RAD methods are most effective when used in conjunction with traditional software planning techniques as outlined in the SDLC.

Source and Object Codes

A software program can take two forms: source code or object code. Source code, also known as program script, is written by a programmer using a scripting language like JavaScript, and is often described as a crystal or white box because it is readable by trained personnel. Source code must be sent through a script interpreter, which compiles a temporary version of the program for use by the computer. The primary disadvantage of a script interpreter is slow execution time. However, through a process known as program compiling, a programmer can increase program speed by converting the source code into object code, which is essentially machine language. Object code is described as a black box because it is undecipherable by humans. A black box has the advantage of being virtually impervious to unauthorized access. Unfortunately, it prevents project personnel from examining the software's internal logic, and necessitates strict management of the software's many versions.

Version Control

Version control and configuration management are techniques for managing and tracking changes to a software program as it is being developed. Version control tracks the smallest revisions in every version of the software and, in doing so, records the internal configuration of the finished program. Various software tools are used to support version control. For instance, poly version control system, or PVCS, relies on a database to track and document each new version of the software. Each time a programmer works on the software, he will access the PVCS database, which will provide him with the newest version of the program. In this way, programmers are always using the most recent version.

Configuration Management

Configuration management assists project management in controlling the final version of the software. Auditors should determine how an organization carries out configuration management, including:

- The client's method for controlling and documenting changes to each version of the software
- The procedures for testing changes
- The person who authorizes the changes

Phase 4

Software is subjected to numerous tests during SDLC phase 4, and auditors should be aware of the various testing methods, which seek to debug and verify the processing accuracy of the software program. One method is functional testing, also known as *validation testing.* It evaluates the software against project requirements and objectives, and determines whether or not the program fulfills its intended purpose. *Regression testing* ensures that recent changes to the software have not hindered its existing functions. It compares the current software version against all previous versions, and retests the effectiveness of internal controls. Other testing methods include the following: *white-box tests; black-box tests; program module tests; performance tests; integrity tests*, which validate processing accuracy; *internal security control tests; sociability tests*, which test the new program's ability to cooperate with existing programs; and *recovery tests*, which ensure that data can be recovered after a system failure.

White-Box Testing

Software is subjected to numerous tests during SDLC phase 4, and auditors should be aware of the various testing methods. For instance, white-box testing, also known as crystal-box testing, examines a program's internal structure (coding) in order to evaluate its internal logic and calculation accuracy. Although this method is common for self-developed software, it can be very expensive and poses legal problems when commercial software is involved.

Black-Box Testing

The most common method, and is used when software coding is undecipherable or the software is commercially purchased. The test is performed by inputting data into the program, and determining if the output matches expectations and fulfills project requirements.

Phase 5

Phase 5, or the *implementation phase*, prepares the new, fully functional software system for organizational use. Implementation involves transferring the appropriate data into the system, obtaining all necessary certifications and accreditations, training users, and *going live* with the new software. An auditor at this phase must ensure the following:

- The system has received all necessary certifications and management accreditations.
- The system is fulfilling organizational objectives with support from quality control procedures, as well as ongoing maintenance and support plans.
- Internal controls are supporting the authorization and implementation of changes to the system.
- The software has received formal management approval at a review meeting before being put into actual production use and moving to the next phase.

The review meeting is attended by both the project sponsor and project manager, who reports on project updates and progress. The meeting also evaluates the final risk analysis, and examines any concerns related to software engineering or system performance.

Certification

Indicates that the software fulfills a certain standard, and is often necessary to function in a particular work environment. Certification is a technical process that involves testing the software against an established reference and verifying the effectiveness of internal controls. Auditors should be wary both of systems with expired certifications and of systems lacking certifications. After the system is certified, it must be accredited through an administrative process.

Accreditation

Given by management, and dictates the appropriate uses of the system, including the locations it should be implemented. Management determines these uses by examining the software's performance.

CHANGEOVER

Also known as *going live or cutting over* occurs during SDLC phase 5. It describes the process of switching from the existing system to the new system, and requires a *migration plan* that incorporates one of the following changeover methods:

- *Parallel operation* – The old system and the new system are run simultaneously until a future date when the old system can be rendered idle. The project team compares output from the new software against output from the old software in order to identify and correct any problems. Parallel operation poses the least risk, but requires the most support since two systems must be maintained.
- *Phased changeover* – The new system is implemented incrementally over a long period of time. This method poses only moderate risk, but still consumes significant resources. Phased changeover is normally reserved for system upgrades.
- *Hard changeover* – The new system completely replaces the old system at a certain cutoff date. This method is the riskiest and requires the highest priority risk mitigation because it can significantly disrupt organizational activity.

PHASE 6

Phase 6, or the *post-implementation phase*, closes out the project and conducts a project management review, which examines performance metrics to ensure that the new software is fulfilling system requirements and generating the benefits predicted in phase 1. Auditors in phase 6 have the following responsibilities:

- Ensuring the system meets organizational objectives
- Comparing system audits logs against operational reports
- Interviewing users to gauge their approval of the system
- Verifying that the system is being properly supported, maintained, and monitored

Organizations should hold annual review meetings to discuss the system's compliance with controls and objectives. It should also monitor for risk events and be prepared to implement response strategies when needed. Management must document and track any influences that might force the organization to change the system. It should also understand the extent to which a system can be changed.

E-COMMERCE

E-commerce describes business transactions that are conducted electronically. There are several types of e-commerce transactions:

- *Business-to-business, or B-to-B* – An organization procures goods or services from a vendor. These transactions include the online handling of activities such as purchasing, payroll, outsourcing, and accounts payable, and are regulated by contracts under federal law.

- *Business-to-government, or B-to-G* – The government procures goods or services from a vendor. These transactions involve the online filing of legal documentation. Vendors must keep their company profiles in the CCR (Central Contractor Registration) database.
- *Business-to-consumer, or B-to-C* – An organization sells products to consumers online, or provides online customer support. Banking, privacy, and credit authorization laws regulate these kinds of transactions.
- *Business-to-employee, or B-to-E* – An organization administers benefits, payroll, and other employee services online. These transactions are subject to privacy laws.

There are numerous security and privacy risks associated with conducting business online; therefore, an IS audit should be performed on each type of e-commerce transaction.

DATABASES

A **database** provides a structured and organized medium for storing information. A **data-oriented database**, or **DODB**, is intended for predictable information; therefore, data entries must conform to a fixed length and format. A DODB separates its program procedures from its information. Examples include Excel spreadsheets and online forms. An **object-oriented database**, or **OODB**, is designed for unpredictable information; consequently, data entries need not conform to a specific length or format. An OODB merges its program procedures and its information within program objects. Each object has a unique way of processing requests and accessing information, and may represent a module of a larger program (such as a physics program with a module that can work equations). Objects are arranged within a hierarchy according to their *object class*.

DATA INTEGRITY TESTING

Databases are only effective if their information is accurate, complete, and consistent. Therefore, information within databases must be subjected to *integrity testing*, which examines relational integrity and referential integrity. *Relational integrity tests* evaluate data accuracy before it is entered into the database. *Referential integrity tests* ensure that that information is consistent and accurate between tables (or references). These tests are especially important for data-oriented databases, which store information in a set of tables; information in one table may reference or relate to information in another table. Referential integrity is maintained through various keys:

- *Primary key* – The first piece of data contained in a table
- *Foreign key* – Data that links multiple tables
- *Candidate key* – Data that is searched by a user

If data is added, updated, or removed in one table, it must be changed in every other table; otherwise, the keys will not be consistent.

Normalization and Transaction Management

Normalization seeks to eliminate any duplications or inconsistencies within the database. It is achieved by ensuring the following:

- Every table has a primary key.
- Each entry field contains unique information.
- Information in one field can be changed without altering other fields. The only exception here would be the primary key.

Transaction management prevents incomplete or failed transactions from being permanently recorded in the database. This type of management relies on a before-image journal and an after-image journal. The *before-image journal* documents the state of the database before a new transaction update is made. The *after-image journal* tracks the new transaction as it occurs. If it fails, the database returns to the before-image. If the transaction goes through, it is removed from the journals.

Decision Support System

When deciding an issue, a user may rely on a decision support system, or a database containing information relevant to the issue in question. Decision support systems find the necessary information using *heuristics* (or a set of program rules), and include three basic categories:

- *Reference by context* – A low-level system with only moderate value; it selects information and answers that are most relevant to the issue
- *Colleague (or associate) level* – Capable of working mundane calculation; however, the bulk of the decision is still left to the user
- *Expert level* – A system written using the knowledge of a person who has been doing decision support work for decades; it may contain over 50,000 data points—five or more times higher than an expert-level system

The following terms related to data support systems:

- *Data mining* is the process of searching data stored within numerous organizational databases, and finding information that correlates most strongly to the issue in question. The goal of data mining is answering questions using the heuristics (or program rules) of the decision support system.
- *Data warehouses* contain information captured from various organizational databases. Data is recorded by taking *snapshots* of databases on a periodic basis—daily, weekly, monthly, etc.
- *Data marts* store information that has been removed from the warehouse through data mining. The decision support system accesses the data mart, gathers the most relevant information, and presents it to the user through graphical program such as a GUI (graphical user interface).

Balanced Scorecard

The goal of the *balanced scorecard* is to eliminate wasteful activities and, in the case of IT, to create better alignment between IT activities and business objectives. A balanced scorecard relies on metrics created from the following organizational objectives: *business processes* (critical success factors, key performance indicators, and business mission); *growth and learning* (organizational growth plans, training that enables workers and employees to fulfill organizational objectives); *financial* (financial and stakeholder goals); and, *customer* (organizational image within marketplace). According to ISACA, an IT balanced scorecard should apply these organizational objectives across the following IT scoring layers:

- *Strategy* – Includes controlling IT spending, creating IT control objectives, training IT employees, and supporting the development of new IT applications
- *Mission* – Includes getting funding for IT projects, providing effective IT services, and identifying future IT needs
- *Metrics* – Should be created from critical success factors and key performance indicators

Balanced scorecards are only effective if they are chosen and implemented by the highest levels of management (CEO or CFO). Every employee should have his or her own scorecard.

Metrics

Metrics are quantifiable standards for evaluating organizational performance. They should correlate to internal controls, and help fulfill the organization's objectives. Metrics represent performance targets, which are aggregated to create a baseline. There are four kinds of metrics for assessing IT performance:

- *Efficiency metrics* evaluate the punctuality of IT services and applications, such as the length of time between help desk access and help desk response.
- *Effectiveness metrics* assess the effectiveness of IT services and applications, such as the number of help desk incidents that were resolved to the user's satisfaction.
- *Impact metrics* measure the number of incidents by category (i.e. amount of viruses, help desk tickets opened and closed over a period of time, etc), and convert that number into a percentage or value.
- *Implementation metrics* determine the number of systems that conform to quality standards, such as the systems possessing the necessary security protocols.

Service-Level Agreement

A service-level agreement (or SLA) is a formal contract between an organization and a vendor. It specifies the desired service, its quality and quantity, coverage periods, and renewal options. An SLA has the following components:

- *Service definition* – Identifies which goods or services the vendor is expected to provide
- *System availability* – Includes the schedule for system uptime and maintenance downtime
- *Cost of service* – Explains billing methods, as well as the process for calculating the cost of services
- *Right to audit* – Grants the organization a right to audit the vendor
- *Personnel qualifications* – Identifies IT support personnel, their training, and how they will be supporting business users
- *Security requirements* – Explains implementation of controls (physical, logical, access, etc.), segregation of duties, and the method for protecting libraries
- *Data integrity* – Details the methods for protecting and backing up data
- *SLA performance reporting* – Defines the metrics that will be used to report progress and how often they will be reported
- *SLA change procedures* – Explains processes for changing services, including cancellation costs

Redundancy and Self-Assessments

The following methods for creating redundancy in information systems and securing data integrity:

- *Alternate routing* is the practice of transmitting data along multiple paths. In this way, data integrity is maintained even if the primary transmission pathway fails. Alternate routing is best suited for WANs and LANs.
- *Mirrored servers* consist of a primary server and a secondary server. If the primary server fails for any reason, the secondary server takes over, thereby preventing any loss of information and preserving data integrity. Mirrored servers are a type of RAID (Redundant Array of Disks) system, which creates redundancy in information systems.

Organizations should conduct *technical self-assessments*, in which they identify any areas of vulnerabilities. Technical self-assessments may be conducted using the following methods developed by the National Security Agency, or NSA: Level 1 information system assessment methodology (IAM) and Level 2 information evaluation methodology (IEM).

Firewalls

Firewalls protect a network against unauthorized access by another network. They can consist of either hardware or software, and can be external or internal to the network. For instance, a firewall can restrict an external network, such as the

Internet, from accessing an organizational network. Or, it can restrict a department from internally accessing another department within the same organization. Firewalls intercept incoming data packets and compare them against a set of access requirements, which are explained in the organization's security policy. Traffic that meets these guidelines is allowed access to the network. Traffic that does not meet guidelines is filtered and/or redirected. A properly configured firewall serves as a gateway, receiving all traffic that wants access to the network and comparing it against access requirements.

Most firewalls evaluate incoming traffic against the following criteria:

- *Protocol* – If an incoming data transmission is using the wrong protocol, the firewall may deny it access to the network.
- *Source and destination address* – Data transmissions with certain destinations and source addresses may be redirected or filtered.
- *Source and destination port* – Firewalls may deny network access if the data transmission is trying to access a certain port or application.

Auditors should ensure their clients are performing the following tasks: using firewalls that have been properly configured; monitoring firewall performance using a set of predefined process and procedures; funneling all network traffic through the firewall; and utilizing both external (perimeter) and internal firewalls. Many organizations neglect internal security because they mistakenly assume that security threats only exist outside the organization.

Limitations

Although a firewall reduces the number of external attacks, it cannot possibly receive and manage all traffic going into the network. Attacks can circumvent firewalls by entering through other access points, such as modems.

Proper Configurations

Also, firewalls are only effective if they are configured properly; therefore, IT administrators should use one of the following three configurations:

- *Screened host implementation* safeguards a single host computer against attack.
- *Dual-homed configuration* is common for Internet firewalls: Two interface cards are installed on the same host computer, which is configured while the router is offline. The cards communicate with each other using special software.
- *DMZ configuration (also known as a screened subnet)* places a group of computers into a protected subnet. This configuration maintains a separation of duties, and allows for redundancy between data systems.

INFORMATION ASSETS SECURITY CONTROLS

Auditors must understand the four types of controls protecting information assets:

- *Systems access controls* restrict access to information systems, and are predicated on the *least privilege* principle, which holds that employees should only be able to access information relevant to their work functions. These controls include user logins, privileged logins, and maintenance logins.
- *Data files controls* prevent unauthorized access to data files by securing the following access points: direct file, perimeter, and middleware (or software that directs data as it travels from the user interface to the database). These include standing data, system control parameters, logical access, and transaction process controls.
- *Application process controls* maintain system security and data integrity. These controls include input, output, and authorization controls.
- *Maintenance controls* prevent disruption to the system when hardware or software changes are made. These include backup, recovery, and project management.

SYSTEM ACCESS CONTROLS

- A user login account is type of system access control in which an ID and password are distributed to each system user. An employee's login should only grant him the minimum level of access needed to complete his job function. Each user login system should possess certain features:
    - Unique passwords consisting of both numbers and letters, and possessing a minimum length of six letters; users should not be able to reuse passwords
    - Suspension of user login account after no more than five login attempts
    - Changing of each password after a maximum of 60 days
    - Audits logs documenting unauthorized personnel who attempt to access the system
    - Notification of when the user's last successful login
    - Warning that criminal prosecution may result from unauthorized access to information; this should be posted before login

  Managers should review suspended login accounts to determine if an unauthorized access had occurred.

- *Privileged login accounts* are reserved for system administrators, who should also possess a conventional login for their daily work functions. Administrators should only access their privileged login account when performing administrative or maintenance duties; for any other work, they should access their regular login account. Privileged login accounts should change passwords every 30 days. Both existing and retired passwords should be documented in hardcopy and electronic formats. Hardcopies should be stored in a secure, fireproof safe in the event of disaster recovery.

- *Maintenance login accounts* grant access for system maintenance and setup. These accounts should possess unique login names, passwords, and station restrictions, which restrict login access to a specific computer workstation. When a system is being developed, it may use a set of well known and easily accessible default maintenance accounts, which the system administrator should deactivate prior to production use.

DATA FILE CONTROLS

- *Standing data controls* prevent unauthorized access to data stored within databases, files, and storage mediums like disk drives. The level of control will depend on the sensitivity of the information, and may include encryption features.
- *Logical access controls* include user rights management programs, which authenticate user rights before access is given. In effect, users must go through an authentication process before they are granted access to data files.
- *Transaction processing controls* authenticate and validate all data transactions by ensuring they receive official approval. These controls may include *transaction process* (or *TP*) *monitors*, which prevent database activity from exceeding hardware requirements.
- *System control parameters* help modify software and configuration settings. IT personnel must be wary and exercise the proper controls when implementing these parameters; otherwise, system performance and security may be adversely affected.

APPLICATION PROCESSING CONTROLS

- *Input controls* prevent data transactions from accepting unauthorized information or processing the same transaction more than once (sequence checks). These controls examine source domain signatures, logins and passwords, and workstation IDs.
- *Output controls* maintain the confidentiality of data until it reaches the user who requested it. There are several types of output controls, including the following:
    - *Event logs* ensure data confidentiality by tracking and documenting processing and audit logs.
    - *Report retention* is the set of policies for the retention of records, such as various regulatory and legal records.
    - *Report generation/distribution controls* prevent sensitive information from being outputted on unauthorized printers. According to these controls, confidential reports must state their confidential nature on the title page, and exception reports must indicate how many exceptions have occurred.
    - *Negotiable instrument controls* use both logical and physical controls to protect financial instruments (such as bonds, stock certificates, and checks) when they are printed out.

- *Processing controls* maintain data accuracy and transaction validity by examining *batches* of data or transactions from the system. Batches can be of any size and obtained over any time period. There are several types of processing controls:
  - *Batch totals* ensure that data input matches processing
  - *Transaction logs* track and document database activities
  - *Exception reporting* finds errors, and may suspend or reject data and transaction batches until the problems are resolved
  - *Total item number* ensure the processing of every item of data
  - *Job cost accounting* evaluates the efficiency of job cost accounting procedures; departments, projects, and applications will be billed individually for computer operating costs
  - *Transactions logs* documents system activity
  - *Limit checks* stops excessively large transactions from being processed
  - *Run-to-run totals* validates data at each processing stage

Processing controls should ensure that access to the library database is limited to read-only.

Maintenance Controls

- *Backup and recovery* – System maintenance should not begin until backup and recovery plans have been implemented. These plans involve copying data and system programs onto media and backup tapes that have been read/write verified. In the event of disaster, these tapes are used to recover any information that was lost.
- *Project management* – Because maintenance is a project, it must utilize project management, including risk analysis and project planning. More extensive maintenance requires more extensive project planning, and vice versa. In some cases, maintenance may be unsuccessful; therefore, the project plan should contain fallback procedures.

Threats and Crimes

Organizations should implement administrative, technical, and physical controls to contend with the following types of threats and crimes:

- *Theft* is more common from internal threats than external threats, because employees generally have greater motive, opportunity, and means.
- *Fraud* is the act of gaining access to organizational resources through misrepresentation.
- *Blackmail* is the attempt to obtain money or resources by threatening an organization. This category of crime includes extortion.
- *Industrial espionage* is the act of spying on an organization to steal its secrets.
- *Sabotage* is the willful and malicious destruction of company property.
- *Loss of credibility* is injury to an organization's reputation.
- *Loss of proprietary information* is the loss of trade secrets due to the mishandling of company information assets.

- *Unauthorized disclosure* involves releasing sensitive information (client records, trade secrets, etc.) without the company's consent.
- *Legal repercussions* can result if the organization loses private client information due to negligence or misconduct.

Hackers

A hacker, also known as a *cracker*, is a computer programmer seeking an unauthorized level of access to an organization's computer network. Hackers may be trying to disrupt regular computer processing or discredit the organization. Their motivations normally involve financial gain, political reasons, personal enmity, or a desire for excitement. Although hackers can be external or internal to the organization, hacking from within may pose the greatest threat; employees normally have the most in-depth knowledge of the strengths and weaknesses of their organization's computer network. Consequently, auditors should always gauge the satisfaction and contentment of employees and workers. Not all hacking is considered criminal behavior; organizations may hire ethical hackers, known as *white hats*, to test the organization's network for possible security breaches.

Passive Attacks

Passive attacks acquire important information by monitoring an organization's computer network. They normally precede active attacks. There are three types of passive attacks:

- *Host traffic analysis* identifies important systems on the network, such as servers. The attacker records the communications activity between host computers, and determines the amount of service requests. A *fingerprinting* tool such as an Nmap can determine the operating system of the host computers.
- *Network analysis* examines computer traffic, and generates a map of the network through a technique known as *footprinting* or *painting*. These maps list the locations of routers and host computers, and are used to coordinate active attacks.
- *Eavesdropping* is the use of special tools to analyze network communication and capture various data files and communiqués (such as emails, Instant Messages, keystrokes, login ID, and passwords) as they traverse the network. Certain eavesdropping tools are capable of breaking encryption codes.

Active Attacks

Active attacks seek to steal organizational resources or disrupt normal network operation. They are coordinated using information gained from passive attacks. There are many types of active attacks, including the following:

- *Viruses:* Self-propagating, multiplying programs capable of permeating many different computers or an entire network. Their sole purpose is interrupting network operations. Computers should contain antivirus software, which detects and quarantines viruses by identifying their behavior (signature scanning), checking integrity, or performing a heuristic scan.
- *Worms* – Highly dangerous programs capable of moving anywhere on the computer network. They take advantage of system weaknesses, and actively locate and move to new systems.
- *Logic bombs* – Destructive programs that lie dormant until they are triggered. Logic bombs are confined to one location. They can be planted intentionally or as an unintended consequence of programming errors.
- *Social engineering* – The act of gaining access by misrepresenting one's identity. In essence, the attacker presents a false persona—normally a programmer, contractor, employee, or someone else of authority—in order to trick another person into giving him access to the network.
- *Phishing* -- A of social engineering in which an attacker distributes false emails to organizational employees, hoping they will click the enclosed link and access the attacker's counterfeit website. The false website attempts to coerce employees into divulging sensitive information, such as passwords, login IDs, important numbers, and bank account information. By acquiring this information, the attacker can download spyware, viruses, and other invasive programs to the computer network.
- *Denial of service (or DoS)* – Occurs when an attacker renders a computer terminal inoperative, essentially shutting down the system. The computer becomes unable to execute basic processing duties.
- *Dumpster diving* – The act of sorting through an organization's garbage for sensitive information. As long as the attacker is not trespassing, dumpster diving is not illegal; therefore, any sensitive information should be destroyed or shredded rather than simply discarded.
- *Trapdoors* – Provide hidden access points to computer software. They are normally installed by the software programmer for purposes of testing and creating shortcuts. Programmers eliminate most trapdoors before the software is put into use. However, a few may remain to help the vendor provide customer support; these trapdoors pose a security risk.
- IP fragmentation – Circumvents the network firewall by transmitting numerous *fragmented* service requests to a computer. An IP fragmentation attack can be thwarted easily by configuring the firewall to reject fragmented requests.

- *Brute force* – A method of attack that brings overwhelming power against a particular control or safeguard. For instance, certain programs determine passwords by comparing the password encryption against all possible matches in a dictionary. This kind of attack can be averted by using passwords that are not included in any dictionary.
- *Crash-restart* – The act of downloading invasive programs that are capable of reconfiguring the security settings of a computer and then crashing the system. After the computer reboots automatically, the new settings take effect, allowing the attacker to create his own backdoor into the software.
- *Salami technique* – A method for conducting illegal financial activity; the attacker steals (or electronically deducts) amounts of money that are small enough to go unnoticed. If the attacker can make enough deductions, he can accrue a large amount without attracting notice.
- *Remote access* – The act of accessing an insecure computer network remotely, usually for personal or political gain. There are two primary types of remote access attacks:
- *War dialing* – Uses an automated modem-dialing tool to randomly call various phone numbers. This is a type of *brute force attack*. If the number is answered by a modem, it will be added to a list. The attacker searches the list for modems that are unsecured. To protect against war dialing, all modems should have firewalls or should be configured to reject inbound calls.
- *War driving or walking* – Attempts to locate insecure wireless access points by driving or walking past wireless network transmitters. Through a practice known as *war chalking*, an attacker may mark the organization's property to alert other attackers that a network is vulnerable through an insecure transmitter. Attacker may even place this information on the Internet.
- *Maintenance accounts* – Facilitate system support. As a feature of many computer systems, they are included in the default settings. In most cases, the IT administrator disables any default maintenance accounts before the system is put into use. However, by tracking unauthorized attempts to access these accounts, IT personnel may be able to predict impending attacks.
- *Cross-network connectivity* – Increases computer processing efficiency. It can be established internally (within the organization) or externally (over the Internet). Businesses often create special connections to communicate with their business partners. Unfortunately, if attackers find these connections, they can exploit the system while evading detection. To effectively avoid the risks associated with cross-network connectivity, an organization must implement both internal and external firewalls.

- *Email spamming* – The act of distributing large quantities of identical emails to numerous users. It is often used in conjunction with *phishing*. Sending out mass quantities of emails is only legal if the sender informs recipients of his address and provides them a means of removing their names from his mailing list.
- *Email spoofing* – The act of misrepresenting the identity of an email and its sender. Its purpose is coercing the recipient into clicking a false link and divulging sensitive information.
- *Packet replay* – The use of a tool such as a network sniffer to capture data packets as they travel through the network. By recording these packets and retransmitting them, an attacker can misrepresent himself as a legitimate sender. Packet replay is frequently used in conjunction with DoS and Kerberos attacks.
- *Source routing* – A special protocol that enables a data transmission to travel through the network while ignoring the network's configuration. By following a set of instructions provided by the sender, a transmission can reach its target destination and simultaneously bypass any network routers and firewalls. Source routing was originally developed for performing diagnostics and communicating with remote networks. Unfortunately, hackers can also gain access to these protocols; therefore, each router must be programmed to ignore them.
- *Message modification* – The act of capturing and altering network transmissions before they reach their destination. In order to appear legitimate, the address or information contained within the modified message is altered before it is retransmitted. Message modification is part of a *man-in-the-middle attack*, in which an attacker (a third party) covertly intercepts messages between two legitimate parties so he can eavesdrop.

Information Security Management

Information security management seeks to maintain the confidentiality, accuracy, and accessibility of data resources. This responsibility involves three primary job positions:

- *Chief security officer (CSO)* – Establishes and enforces the organization's security policy. This position holds the highest authority level, but tends to be more formal than functional.
- *Chief privacy officer (CPO)* – Maintains the confidentiality of client and employee information. This position is subordinate only to the CSO but, once again, tends to be mainly formal.
- *Information systems security manager (ISSM)* – Oversees the information system security analysts, establishes daily priorities, and makes certain that the organization is following security procedures. The ISSM implements the policies of the CPO and CSO, and manages a group of information systems security analysts, or ISSAs, who handle security issues on a case-by-case basis.

Classification Levels for Information

An important aspect of IT security governance is categorizing information according to its importance and sensitivity. Information is generally categorized in the following levels:

- *Confidential* – The highest security level for information, and is often subdivided into confidential and highly confidential. This includes trade secrets, buyout negotiations, and specifics about an organization's internal operations.
- *Private (internal use only)* – Applied to operating procedures and employment records (health care information, salary data, employee performance reviews, etc.).
- *Sensitive* – Includes any document whose disclosure is limited to select groups but may be part of public or legal record. Client and vendor lists, pricing plans, and contract terms are some examples.
- *Public* – Includes any information intended for public disclosure, such as advertisements, websites, and any other documented filed at the courthouse. This information should undergo substantial editing.

Context and Data Retention

Context describes the manner in which information is used, and helps determine the security classification for a piece of data. If an organization fails to classify its information, it invites two major risks: Information mishandling and intense legal scrutiny during proceedings.

Data retention involves procedures for determining the correct method for storing data, the length of time data should be stored, and the proper method for archiving or disposing of data. When creating retention procedures for a specific type of data, an organization will consider the following criteria: the data's value to the organization, the period over which it is useful, and any laws surrounding its usage and retention.

Physical Access Threats

Auditors should identify who has been granted physical access to IT systems, acquire a map of all access routes, and determine if the proper controls (locks, physical controls, guards, etc.) are in place. These controls maintain server and network security, and should be implemented over three primary types of physical access points:

- *Sensitive areas* – Include locations such as computer rooms and wiring closets. If an attacker acquires unregulated access to these areas, he can damage equipment, bypass logical controls, or install listening devices.

- *Service ports* – Include the maintenance ports on routers, servers, and other types of network equipment. With access to these ports, an attacker can bypass security passwords, short out equipment, and acquire password and login IDs by hacking the computer's memory.
- *Computer console* – The server's keyboard. Without safeguards or highly regulated access, a console can be used to shut down the entire system or to hack into disk drives.

Physical Protection

Physical protection includes any barriers or controls designed to regulate physical access routes to the IT system. The auditor should perform a risk assessment to determine if the level of physical protection is effective and sufficient. There are several types of physical controls and barriers, including the following:

- *Closed-circuit television* – Monitors activity and access routes in real-time, and contributes to audit logs. Monitoring equipment should provide good image quality and a retention capacity that allows security personnel to view activity from previous weeks.
- *Security guards* – Notice details that others might overlook. When complemented by closed-circuit television, they can monitor distant areas and numerous areas simultaneously. They can also handle unique events in ways that computers cannot.
- *Burglar alarms* – Alert security personnel when a physical barrier (such as a door or window) has been breached. An appropriate response can only be implemented if the alarm is being monitored.
- *Traditional tumbler lock* – An inexpensive type of lock that uses a simple brass key. Tumbler locks require minimal effort to install, but provide no way of identifying the persons who have accessed the lock.
- *Electronic lock* – Uses a badge reader to grant access. Because each badge possesses a unique ID number assigned to a specific person, electronic locks can track the people who have accessed it. However, there is no way to track the number of people who passed through the door while it was open.
- *Cipher lock* – Grants access when a person enters the correct combination into a keypad. In a low-security environment, everyone may use the same combination. In a high-security environment, each person possesses a unique combination.
- A *biometric* – A type of unique locking mechanism that grants access on the basis of a specific human characteristic (such as finger or palm prints, retina scans, voice recognition, etc.).

Technical Protection

Technical (or logical) protection restricts data access. It is implemented through hardware or software, and includes the following types of technical (or automated) controls:

- *Mandatory access controls (or MACs)* label pieces of data according to their security classification. Users can only gain access to data if their access level matches the data's security label.
- *Discretionary access controls (or DACs)* are very common among businesses, and are implemented at the discretion of the data owner. He alone decides which users are allowed access to his data. Auditors should evaluate the data owner's process for reviewing data and authorizing access to it.
- *Role-based access controls (or RBACs)* grant data access according to the user's job function. In effect, the user is only granted access to data if it is absolutely necessary to complete his job function.

Identification and Authentication

When a user is trying to gain access to certain data systems or information, he must follow two processes. The first process is known as *identification*, in which the user makes known his identity. The next process is *authentication*, in which the user's identity is confirmed and verified for access to the system. Authentication can be confirmed based on three types of information:

- *Type 1: login ID and password* – Each user possesses a unique password and ID.
- *Type 2: unique item in user's possession* – In addition to a password and ID, the system verifies user identify on the basis of a unique item in the user's possession, such as an ID card, hard token, or USB token.
- *Type 3: biometrics* – Access is granted based on specific physical characteristics of the user, such as fingerprints, hand geometry, or facial scans.

Biometrics

- *Fingerprints* are commonly used to authenticate a user's identity. In most cases, the biometrics database does not use an actual fingerprint image for authentication; instead, it uses *minutiae,* such as the position, curvature, delta, ride patterns, combined ridges, burification, or islands of the user's fingerprint.
- *Palm print authentication* is very similar to the finger print method. It authenticates the user according to the minutiae of his palm print.
- *Hand geometry* is an efficient and economical means of authenticating identity. A three-dimensional image of the user's hand is recorded and stored in the biometrics database.
- A *face scan* is a three-dimensional image of the positioning of the user's facial features, such as his nose, mouth opening, and eye sockets.

- *Iris scans* authenticate users according to the characteristics of their irises, such as the rings, freckles, and furors in the eye's pupil. A camera scans the iris of the user, and compares against it against the image stored in the biometric database.
- *Retina scans* record the vein and artery patterns located behind the user's eyeball. Retina scanning is a very effective means of authenticating users, but raises a number of privacy issues; changes in the retina can indicate medical problems.
- *Voice patterns* are the unique characteristics of the user's voice, such as its speed, tone, and inflection. Although inexpensive, voice pattern recognition systems suffer from accuracy problem because they can be fooled by tape recordings.
- *Signature dynamics* record the pressure, time duration, and technique with which users write their signatures. Using special software, the system authenticates users by having them rewrite their signatures each time they want access.

Errors Present in Biometric Systems

Biometric systems pose a number of problems. They often encounter resistance from users who feel their privacy is being violated, or who have concerns about the cleanliness of such a system. Consequently, organizations must create and implement policies regulating the manner in which biometric data is collected, processed, distributed, and kept confidential. These policies should also address the following kinds of errors:

- *Enrollment errors* occur when the biometric system rejects a sample provided by the user. Every system user must provide a biometric sample. The sampling (enrollment) process should last no longer than five minutes.
- *False acceptance errors (also known as type 2 errors)* occur when the system authenticates the wrong user, granting him a level of system access that he should not have.
- *False rejection errors (also known as type 1 errors)* occur when the system rejects a user who should be granted access.
- *Equal error rate (also known as crossover error rate)* should never exceed the acceptable error rate for the biometric system.

Kerberos Single Sign-on System

The Kerberos single sign-on system is a security system implemented when destination points (i.e., computers and servers) are considered secure but the transmission pathway (i.e., network) is vulnerable. Kerberos is only effective with highly specialized software and experienced systems administrators; otherwise, there may be compatibility problems. Logging into a Kerberos system involves four steps:

1. The user sends his authentication to Kerberos.
2. The workstation terminal sends its authentication to Kerberos.

3. Kerberos establishes a network access ticket, and uses a shared encryption key.
4. The workstation terminal receives the Kerberos access ticket via the shared encryption key, and is subsequently signed in to all network servers (which also receive access tickets from Kerberos).

The user is allowed to sign in to all network servers.

Virtual Private Network

Through a virtual private network, users can gain remote access and transmit data over a secure and inexpensive connection. A VPN is established using the Internet or similar insecure public network, and can be used to link two computers, a computer and a network, or two networks. VPN uses the following types of protocols and/or technology:

- Point-to-point tunneling protocol (PPTP)
- Layer 2 tunneling protocol (L2TP) is established at OSI layer 2.
- *Secure sockets layers (SSL)* are established at OSI layer 5. It creates a one-way, secure transaction between user and server while maintaining data integrity. The user logs in to the servers through a Secure Shell (SSH).
- *IP security (IPSec) Internet protocol* is established at OSI layer 3. IPSec can be established in two ways: *transport mode*, which encrypts the payload, and *tunnel mode*, which encrypts both payload and network address.

IDS

An intrusion detection system (IDS) alerts the administrator when there is an unauthorized attempt to access the network. Newer versions of the IDS, such as the intrusion prevention system (IPS), can actual block the attack as soon as it is detected. An IDS is only effective if it is continuously monitored. There are two primary types of IDS:

- *Host-based systems* monitor a specific network device or computer; consequently, they are incapable of detecting network incursions through other devices or computers.
- *Network-based systems* are attached to a certain network link, and monitor all activity passing through the connection. In most cases, network IDSs are reserved for the most-used network connections.

Technical Types of Intrusion Detection Systems (IDSS)

An intrusion detection system (IDS) can use three technical methods for detecting a network intrusion:

- The *signature method* compares network activity against a database of known attack methods. Upon discovering a match, the IDS alerts the system administrator of a possible attack.

- The *statistical method* uses a statistical model based on network traffic, CPU, and memory loading to identify possible network attacks. This method is prone to false alarms, but can detect new methods that might not appear in a database.
- The *neural method* combines both signature and statistical methods. A neural IDS is capable of learning.

Some IDSs provide decoy targets designed to entice the attention of hackers and reveal possible threats. These decoys serve no genuine business purpose, and include *honey pots*, which are fake servers, and *honey nets*, which are fake subnets.

Encryption Systems

The first encryption method is the *private-key system,* which uses symmetric cryptography. In essence, the sender and receiver of the message share a single secret key with two parts. Using mathematical algorithms, the first part scrambles and unscrambles the message, while the second part randomizes the encryption process. Longer keys create more security, and vice versa. Private keys work very quickly, because both the sender and receiver are using the same key. Unfortunately, because they pose a number of security risks, they cannot be used with digital signatures.

The second encryption method is the *public-key system,* which uses asymmetrical cryptography. It relies on two encryption keys—a secret key and a public key, which can be distributed to anyone. Encrypting the message requires the public and private keys of the sender as well as the public key of the receiver. Decrypting the message requires the public and private keys of the receiver. Public keys can be used with digital signatures.

Digital Signatures and Cryptography

A *digital signature* is unique to a specific person, much like a written signature. A sender attaches his own digital signature to data transmissions before sending them to their recipients, who confirm the signature using the message file and public key of the sender. *Elliptic-curve cryptography* is popular with wireless devices. An elliptic encryption key is a random point in a three-dimensional space generated by the technology, and is far more difficult to crack than linear algorithms. *Quantum cryptography* is an experimental technology that relies on the polarization effects associated with random photonic bursts. Although the technology is very promising, it has yet to be made commercially available. Auditors should evaluate the organization's methods for producing, storing, controlling, and disposing of encryption keys. Organizations should be protecting keys from theft, and using a different key for each purpose.

Public-Key Infrastructure

Using a public key infrastructure (PKI), multiple users can share encrypted files, and verify file authenticity by checking digital certificates. PKIs consist of the following four parts:

- Certification authority (CA) distributes digital certificates to users. Any data file sent by the user will contain his digital certificate, which includes contact information as well as a number of additional characteristics that are unique to the user.
- Registration authority (RA) is a department of a big company. It possesses a block of digital certificates, which have been acquired from a certification authority. The RA can issue certificates, but the CA still maintains them.
- The certification revocation list (CRL) documents the certificates that have been expired, revoked, or cancelled.
- The certification practice statement (CPS) explains the CA's procedures for issuing, revoking, using, and controlling digital certificates.

E-Commerce Security Protocols

The following network security protocols help ensure the safety of e-commerce transactions:

- *IPSec* is an IP security protocol at OSI layer 3.
- *TLS* provides transport layer security at OSI layer 4.
- *HTTPS* secures hypertext at OSI layer 5.
- *SSL* stands for secure sockets layer, and applies at OSI layer 5.
- *PGP* provides security for personal data encryption at OSI layer 7.
- *Secure electronic transaction, or SET,* is a protocol that protects credit transactions over the Internet. In effect, a person can use his credit card to pay an online vendor without ever disclosing his credit card numbers.
- *S/MIME, or Secure Multipurpose Internet Mail Extension,* ensures the security and integrity of emails and email attachments, and allows the recipient to authenticate the message.

Organizational Structure

There are five types of organizational structure: functional, projectized, weak matrix, strong matrix, and balanced matrix. Each one has its own advantages and disadvantages, and allots its project managers and auditors varying levels of authority.

- *Functional organizations* are divided into various departments and are ideal for routine projects. Project managers have very little authority; instead, most of the power resides with functional managers. This type of power structure has a number of disadvantages: it often hinders project managers from acquiring the necessary resources for their projects, and forces projects to function without adequate managerial authority. Project managers usually have titles such as coordinator, expediter, or project leader.

- *Projectized organizations* are divided into projects rather than departments. Project managers are highly empowered and can dictate project direction with almost complete autonomy. This type of power structure is advantageous because it increases access to resources and facilitates communication within the project. However, a number of disadvantages exist as well. Project managers are judged solely by a project's success or failure; consequently, managers tend to stockpile resources, creating competition with other managers. Professional growth within a projectized organization is severely limited because positions within the company are discontinued once the project is completed. Also, team members may become distracted towards the end of a project due to uncertainty and concern about future employment.

A *matrix* organizational structure combines elements of functional structures with elements of projectized structures.

- *Weak matrix* – Project managers have very limited authority and are subject to functional managers; consequently, project managers often lack the power to acquire resources.
- *Balanced matrix* – Project managers and functional managers split power evenly, leading to competition for resources.
- *Strong matrix* – Project managers are given a high level of authority for a limited duration of time. This type of power structure facilitates resource acquisition and improves communication between team members; however, because project managers often compete for resources amongst themselves, certain projects may not function efficiently due to poor resource distribution.

Review Video: Corporate Organizational Structure
Visit mometrix.com/academy and enter code: 752986

Project Management

Project management involves fulfilling project requirements by applying certain skills and processes. Because many of these skills and processes are also used in auditing, auditors should possess a thorough understanding of project management. Effective project management requires one to balance the three key demands that pertain to every project:

- *Cost* – How much will the project cost?
- *Scope* – What are the project's goals and objective?
- *Time* – When will the project be completed?

Effective project managers fulfill the project's scope without exceeding its cost and time constraints. Similarly, auditors should be able to meet the audit's goals in a certain amount of time and within a predefined budget. Balancing these demands may require meeting and negotiating with stakeholders, who include any person—external or internal to the organization—with an interest in the project.

Project Cycle and Phase

The *project life cycle* includes all the phases, processes, and schedule activities undertaken during the lifetime of a particular project. The organization creates and defines the project life cycle for the sole purpose of meeting stakeholder demands. A *project phase* is a constituent of the lifecycle and the project. Created by the organization, a project phase produces a quantifiable deliverable and includes a review at the end. According to PMI, all process can be classified under five different process groups:

- *Initiating processes* occur early in the project's lifecycle. They define the scope and authorize the project.
- *Planning processes* document project scope, goals, and objectives.
- *Executing processes* generate deliverables and exhaust most of the project's resources.
- *Monitoring and controlling processes* evaluate project performance and manage changes to the project.
- *Closing processes* finish the project.

Knowledge Areas

PMI also classifies processes according to nine *knowledge areas:* integration management, scope management, time management, cost management, quality management, human resource management, communications management, risk management, and procurement management.

Scope Management

The project scope management knowledge area includes the definition of the eventual outcome (i.e. good or service) of the project as well as the work necessary to reach that outcome. It includes the following processes:

- *Scope planning* is the process of creating the scope management plan, and is part of the planning process group.
- *Scope definition* is the process of creating the scope statement, and is part of the planning process group.
- *Creation of WBS (Work Breakdown Structure)* is the process of creating the WBS and WBS dictionary, and is part of the planning process group.
- *Scope verification* is the process of generating accepted deliverables, and is part of the monitoring and controlling process group.
- *Scope control* is the process of generating project scope updates, and is part of the monitoring and controlling process group

Integration

Change occurs frequently throughout a project's lifetime, and changes to one process often create changes to other processes. The project integration management knowledge area includes the following processes, which help manage and implement changes across the entire project:

- *Developing the project charter* is part of the initiating process group.
- Developing the preliminary scope statement is part of the initiating process group.
- *Developing the project management plan* is part of the planning process group.
- *Directing and managing the project execution* produces deliverables such as work results, and is part of the executing process group.
- *Monitoring and controlling project work* generates recommended actions, corrective actions, and change requests, and is part of the monitoring and controlling process group.
- *Integrated change control* generates approved changes requests, and is part of the monitoring and controlling process group.
- *Closing the project* entails archiving project results, and is part of the closing process group.

Time Management

The project time management knowledge area includes the identification and management of the activities and resources necessary to complete the project. It includes the following processes:

- *Activity definition process* is the process of creating the activity list, and is part of the planning process group.
- *Activity sequencing* is the process of generating network diagrams, and is part of the planning process group.
- *Activity resource estimating* is the process of determining resource requirements, and is part of the planning process group.
- *Activity duration estimating* is part of the planning process group.
- *Schedule development* is part of the planning process group.
- *Schedule control* is the process of generating schedule updates, and is part of the monitoring and controlling process group.

Resource Management

The project human resource management knowledge area includes the identification and documentation of the human resources necessary for project completion (such as project staff) and the definition of their roles and responsibilities. It includes the following processes:

- *Human resource planning* is the process of identifying roles and responsibilities, and is part of the planning process group.
- *Acquiring the project team* is the process of staffing the project, and is part of the executing process group.

- *Developing the project team* is the process of improving project performance by honing the skills and communication of the project team, and is part of executing process group.
- *Managing the project team* is the process of generating changes requests and corrective actions, and is part of the monitoring and controlling process group.

Cost Management

The project cost management knowledge area includes the determination and management of project costs, using methods such as the earned value technique. It contains the following processes:

- *Cost estimating* is part of the planning process group.
- *Cost budgeting* is the process of calculating the cost baseline, and is part of the planning process group.
- *Cost control* is the process of generating budget updates, and is part of the monitoring and controlling process group.

Quality Management

The project quality management knowledge area includes the definition of the quality requirements of the project, the auditing of project performance, and the inspection of the project's results against the quality requirement. This knowledge area includes the following processes:

- *Quality planning* is the process of documenting the quality management plan, and is part of the planning process group.
- *Performing quality assurance* is the process of improving project quality by applying quality standards, and is part of the executing process group.
- *Performing quality control* is the process of determining whether or not the project's product fulfills quality standards, and is part of monitoring and controlling.

Procurement Management

The project procurement management knowledge area contains processes that are used when a project must procure resources from vendors outside the organization. The following processes identify, document, and acquire resources:

- *Planning purchases and acquisitions* is the process of creating the procurement management plan by determining which products must be procured, and is part of the planning process group.
- *Plan contracting* is the process of determining the method by which products will be procured, and is part of the planning process group.
- *Requesting seller responses* is the process of distributing documents to potential vendors, and is part of the executing process group.

- *Selecting sellers* is the process of choosing vendors and creating contracts, and is part of the monitoring and controlling process group.
- *Contract administration* is the process of monitoring vendor work, and is part of the monitoring and controlling process group.
- *Contract closure* is the process of formally accepting vendors' work and closing the contract, and is part of the closing process group.

Communications Management

The project communications management knowledge area includes the identification of the informational needs of stakeholders and the management of communication with stakeholders, and includes the following processes:

- *Communication planning* is the process of creating the communications management plan by identifying the informational needs of stakeholders, and is part of the planning process group.
- *Information distribution* is the process of managing communication with stakeholders, and is part of the executing process group.
- *Performance reporting* is the process of creating project performance reports using earned value technique, and is part of the monitoring and controlling process group.
- *Managing stakeholders* is the process of addressing any problems with stakeholder communications, and is part of the monitoring and controlling process group.

Risk Management

The project risk management knowledge area identifies and examines potential risks to the project, and creates response plans for every identified risk. Risk management includes the following processes:

- *Risk management planning* is part of the planning process group.
- *Risk identification* is the process of creating the risk register, and is part of the planning process group.
- *Qualitative risk analysis* is the process of determining the probability a risk may occur and its impact on the project. It is part of the planning process group.
- *Qualitative risk analysis* is the process of predicting the most likely outcomes of risks, and is part of the planning process group.
- *Risk response planning* is the process of determining response plans for identified risks, and is part of the planning process group.
- *Risk monitoring and control* is the process of monitoring for identified risks and identifying new risks, and is part of the monitoring and controlling process group.

Types of Planning

Companies rely on three different types of planning:

- *Strategic plans* last between 3 and 5 years, with the goal of implementing some long-term organizational strategy. They determine the type of business the company runs as well as the company's intention to grow. The primary goal of strategic planning is implementing organizational objectives, which are necessary in fulfilling the goals set by executive management.
- *Long-term plans* last between 1 and 3 years, and determine the specific focus of the business, including its goods and services, management setup, financial plans, and marketing prospects.
- *Operational plans* last 1 year or less, and determine the activities that must be undertaken to fulfill company goals and plan in the short term. Operational plans generate assumptions, responsibilities, change requests, the periodical budget, and production constraints.

Policies

Policies are essential in carrying out a high-level (strategic) plan because they support specific organizational objectives. Using policies, executive management communicates its directives to subordinates, often supported by explicit standards. There are three types of policies:

- *Regulatory* policies require compliance with all applicable laws. The organization may face legal action if its personnel or departments fail to comply.
- *Advisory* policies forbid certain actions or conditions, and explains the ramifications if the person fails to comply. For instance, an advisory policy may forbid an employee from taking excessive breaks. If he fails to comply, he may face punitive measures.
- *Informational* policies communicate the organization's operating policies to the general public. These policies may include a customer refund policy, guarantee of certain behavior or treatment, etc.

Protection of Information Assets

Disaster Recovery

Disaster recovery is the process of rebuilding an organization after a natural or manmade calamity. Natural disasters normally are due to weather conditions, while manmade disasters are the product of poor leadership, operational failure, and inadequate responses to risk events. A disaster recovery plan should implement special procedures designed to avoid the following events:

- Breaking any important contracts
- Cancellation of orders by clients
- Placing new demands on or increasing the responsibilities of business partners
- Rapid sell-off of company stock by investors
- Higher interest rates and/or the immediate calling of business loans by the banker

Business Continuity

The goal of *business continuity* is generating additional revenue for the organization even when it is not creating a product. Business continuity plans can have several possible goals: rebuilding after a disaster (i.e., disaster recovery), bettering the company's position in the marketplace, obtaining or selling off parts of a business, attracting more clients, or changing to a different market. No matter its purpose, a business continuity plan should enable the organization to operate with a minimal amount of resources, interruptions, and decisions needed during a crisis situation. The plan should include the following ten phases:

- Phase 1: Initiation
- Phase 2: Risk analysis
- Phase 3: Business impact analysis
- Phase 4: Create strategy
- Phase 5: Emergency response
- Phase 6: Plan creation
- Phase 7: Training and awareness
- Phase 8: Maintain & test
- Phase 9: Communications
- Phase 10: Integration

Phase 1

Phase 1, or the *initiation phase*, has the following goals: creating a project charter, finding project sponsors, determining the total amount they are willing to pay, defining project scope, identifying business objectives, and documenting the predicted project outcome. Business objectives include *critical success factors* (*CSFs*) and *key performance indicators* (*KPIs*). CSFs are informational needs that must be fulfilled; otherwise, organizational operations could be completely undermined. KPIs measure the performance of a specific project element. Unfortunately, they tend to identify threats only after they become serious problems. A business continuity plan is only successful with top-down sponsorship and planning support from both the IT steering committee and executive management; consequently, the business continuity/disaster recovery planner must convince management of the plan's benefits as well as the many types of threats that could escalate without a plan in place. Business management plans become more attractive if they reveal new ways of increasing organizational revenue.

PHASE 2

Phase 2 is the *risk analysis phase.* The business continuity planner compiles a list of every known threat to the organization, prioritizes them according to their likelihood of occurrence, impact, and dependency, and presents his findings to executive management. Threat categories include but are not limited to natural disasters, manmade disasters, potential risks at the current worksite, potential risks at the alternate worksite, risks associated with relocating, vendor problems, and technological problems. Each category will be subdivided into specific risks, each of which is given a priority ranking. These individual rankings are then aggregated into a total score for the threat category. Each ranking should be based on verifiable evidence that the planner has documented and can reproduce. A planner should take special care when selecting alternate worksites and identifying relocation threats. He should consider the geographic characteristics of each site, such as its crime rate; weather conditions; proximity to major roadways, railways, and cities; municipal services; and access to airports).

THREATS ADDRESSED BY THE BUSINESS CONTINUITY PLAN

Business continuity plans are designed to prevent certain types of threats from escalating during a crisis period. These threat categories include the following:

- *Financial control failures* (such as SEC and banking rules violations, fraud, cash and credit mishandling, and inadequate financial records)
- *Inadequate strategic planning* (such as ineffective marketing, poor public image, and legal changes)
- *Technical asset failure* (brought about by adverse weather conditions, damaged equipment, natural wear, etc.)
- *Operational error* (any kind of human error, including implementing incorrect procedures, poor decision making, insufficient training, group infighting, and poor communication)
- *Poor customer relationships* (such as losing important suppliers, enduring embarrassing events within the organization, and losing customers)

PHASE 3

Phase 3 is the *business impact analysis (BIA) phase*, and is the most significant part of business continuity planning. A BIA maps out the specific operations of an organization by performing the following activities:

- Interviewing and observing organizational personnel as they go about their daily activities
- Evaluating organizational processes by examining process documentation and observing the process as it is being carried out
- Asking a set of questions (similar to BPR questions) in order to determine trigger events and the organization's workflow sequence
- Finding *workarounds* and alternate methods when a business continuity situation arises
- Determining which materials are most important in business recovery (Materials such as records, backup disks, vendor and customer lists, procedures documentation, legal documentation, contracts, and contract data are very important here.)
- Ensuring that CSFs are still valid and being maintained

PHASE 4

Phase 4 is the *strategy selection phase*. The business continuity planner selects a survival strategy based on information gathered in the previous three phases (initiation, risks analysis, and BIA), as well as the plan's ultimate goal (growth, change, or protection). The risk analysis determines the worst-case scenario, while the BIA enables the planner to identify the critical path, which is used to classify each process into three basic categories:

- *Core processes* are absolutely necessary to generate revenue.
- *Supporting processes* directly support revenue generation.
- *Discretionary processes* include all remaining processes. Organizations seldom protect discretionary processes, because they produce minimum value.

Once processes have been classified, the planner should arrange all business continuity activities within timelines that designate the following levels of data recovery: RTO, MAO, RPO, and SDO.

RECOVERY POINT OBJECTIVE (RPO)

The recovery point objective (RPO) is the acceptable amount of data loss after an interruption. In effect, any information inputted between an RPO and the time at which the system goes offline will be lost. RPOs are determined by the type of function:

- *Critical functions* must be completed in order to fulfill core processes. They must be recovered in a very short amount of time; otherwise, the organization may suffer serious damage. They cannot be recovered manually.

- *Vital functions* are less important in fulfilling core processes. Manual recovery may be possible, and recovery times are longer.
- *Sensitive functions* can be recovered manually or simply outsourced. Days can pass before recovery becomes necessary.
- *Non-critical functions* can be permanently discontinued. Recovery is optional.

RTO, MAI and SDO

The *recovery time objective (RTO)* designates a time at which the system should be back online following a disaster. There are normally several RTOs designated as RTO1, RTO2, etc. The *maximum acceptable outage (MAO)* indicates a certain length of time. If a particular system is offline for a period of time exceeding the MAO, the organization may sustain damage. MAO is also known *maximum tolerable downtime*, or *MTD*. The *service delivery objective (SDO)* indicates when a certain group of services becomes available. For instance, at SDO1, customers may be able to access specific services. When the customer moves to SDO2, they may gain access to additional services. SDOx indicates that every service is available.

Continuity Plan Criteria

Organizational management will appoint an executive to activate the business continuity plan when certain criteria are present. These criteria are usually determined by the following events:

- Failure of a marketing campaign
- Success of marketing campaign
- Sustaining a certain amount of physical damage or injury
- Significant dip in production
- Damage to the organization's public image
- Before implementing the plan, the organization must determine an implementation strategy and method. The strategy is determined by resource availability and the requirements imposed by RTO, RPO, and SDO. One implementation method involves *redundant hardware.* It entails the use of two different companies to provide the same service in the event that one fails:
    - *Mirrored servers* consist of two servers functioning as one. The second server assumes full control if the first one fails.
    - *Mirrored disk drives* incorporate RAID technology.
    - *Redundant communication*

Alternate Processing Location

An alternate processing location is used if the primary location fails. There are several kinds of alternate processing location:

- A cold site is the cheapest and least effective alternative. Because cold sites provide little more than a basic structure and no computing equipment, they require weeks to perform recovery; therefore, they are reserved for non-critical functions.
- A warm site is a structure containing basic utilities. It requires days to perform recovery.
- A hot site contains all necessary computing equipment and utilities, which are kept off-line until needed. Hot sites can recover data files and applications in a matter of hours.
- A redundant site is the most expensive alternative, as it contains equipment that is identical to the primary site and is kept in continuous operation. Recovery is possible in seconds, with little or no interruption.
- A mobile site can contain any amount of equipment, and can be moved to the primary location site. Recovery is normally possible within hours or days.

Reciprocal Agreement

Under a reciprocal agreement, two organizations agree to support each other in order to save money and provide assistance during a disaster. In real-world application, reciprocal agreements tend to be impractical due to resource constraints within organizations, security concerns, and competition issues. Also, such agreements cannot be enforced.

Fortification

Fortification involves structurally reinforcing a building to withstand natural and manmade disasters. This can be an expensive process, and the fortification may prove ineffective against flooding, biological or chemical toxins, and many other disasters.

Supply Stockpiles

Supply stockpiles normally include spare parts, office supplies, and enough consumables to last 30 days. Stockpiles are often stored at off-site facilities for use during disaster recovery.

Data Backup Strategy

A data backup strategy involves copying daily information onto disks and tapes that are controlled by a librarian. This strategy is determined by RTO and RPO requirements, and involves one of the following methods:

- *Full backup method* – Each and every system file is copied onto a disk or tape. This method is extremely time-consuming but highly effective.
- *Incremental method* – A file is only copied if it was changed after the previous backup. The incremental method is less time-consuming than a full backup, but requires more time to restore a particular file. This is because the organization must download the full backup as well as each incremental backup.
- *Differential method* – A file is copied each time it is altered between full backups. This is the most common method, because it creates multiple copies of daily files.

Insurance

Business continuity plans often include insurance, which provides financial protection in the event of some kind of loss. There are several types of insurance:

- *Property insurance* covers the financial loss resulting from damage to organizational property.
- *Machinery insurance* protects against the accidental loss of any kind of machinery and/or equipment. This is also known as *boiler insurance.*
- *Casualty insurance* provides financial protection in the event of physical injury, such as worker's compensation.
- *Omission and error insurance* protects against losses associated with administrative errors or omissions.
- *Fidelity insurance/bonding* covers the financial loss associated with employees stealing or embezzling money from the organization.
- *Business interruption insurance* protects against profit loss caused by property damage or loss. It normally pays an organization's fixed operating costs and nothing else.

A number of risks are associated with insurance; the insurance company may try to delay payments or deny them altogether. Also, the insurance policy may not cover all items.

Phase 5

Phase 5 is the *emergency response phase.* The business continuity planner develops and documents a set of emergency response procedures designed to handle *incidents,* which are any events capable of harming organizational resources (people, equipment, and property). These procedures should include the following information: the person responsible for activating the response plan; a set of criteria under which the response plan must be activated; written procedures and decision trees that aid decision making; a list of emergencies and their corresponding responses (including procedures for reporting, safety, situation assessment, and restoration); the circumstances under which the alternate production site should be activated; integration of business continuity, disaster recovery, and response procedures so that everyone is focused on identical goals and objectives; implementation of the Incident Command System (ICS) and all corresponding roles; and, procedures that develop roles, authority, and communication methods for emergency situations.

Incident Command System (ICS)

The Incident Command System (ICS) includes international standards for controlling and managing emergencies. Business continuity planners should implement the following ICS standards, roles, and duties:

- The *incident commander* (*IC*) directs and manages the emergency response team from a field command post at the disaster site, and updates the EOC with crisis command reports.
- The *emergency operations center* (*EOC*) houses the emergency management team (EMT), who chooses a course of action based on reports and recommendations from the IC. The EMT communicates with stakeholders and any part of the business that is unaffected, and appoints a public information office (PIO) to communicate with the media.
- Standards and procedures to establish and secure the EOC
- *Set of conflict resolutions procedures* to work with the various authority figures who will be arriving at the site

Phase 6

During phase 6, also known as the *plan creation phase,* the business continuity plan is created, preferably using a modular design and format for ease of updating and access. The purpose of the plan is directing personnel to the appropriate work locations and explaining their specific work duties in the event of a crisis. Most plans contain the following information: brief executive summary of the plan's purpose and scope; list of emergency responses; procedures for protecting human life; procedures for safeguarding assets and vital documents; ICS standards, roles, and duties (especially the persons in charge); restoration and recovery plans; diagrams, pictures, and flowcharts explaining all required tasks and procedures; logistics intended to maintain event records, keep track of the emergency budget, and support the response teams through housing, food, transportation, and sanitation; and a list of all required teams (emergency response team, management team, salvage team, etc.). In some cases, RTO and SDO requirements cannot be met without acquiring additional personnel.

Phases 7 and 8

During phase 7, the *training and awareness phase*, organizational personnel are taught about the plan and the specific tasks for which they are responsible.

Phase 8 is the *maintain and test phase.* Each process in the business continuity plan undergoes thorough testing, starting with the core processes. Testing should begin with the smaller processes and culminate in the large functional processes. Phase 8 involves the following tests:

- *Desktop review*, or *paper exercise* – Reviews every piece of documentation for consistency errors. This exercise is the first line of testing.
- *Functional tests*, or *modular exercise* – Evaluates procedures as they are being performed, and provides an excellent opportunity for training. This is the second line of testing, and is carried out by an evaluator, who identifies areas needing improvement and ensures that all major processes are receiving the necessary support.
- *Preparedness simulation* – Subjects personnel to various hypothetical scenarios, and determines if they are capable of responding.

PHASE 9

Phase 9 is the *crisis communications phase.* The business continuity planner creates a system for continuous communication with stakeholders, suppliers, clients, owners, and the public during times of crisis. He may also need to set up trauma counseling for organizational personnel and their families. Effective crisis communication entails the following:

- A *prioritized call tree* lists telephone numbers of all personnel who should be informed of the crisis situation. The numbers are called according to priority, and delivered a brief message with instructions.
- *Employee check-in aids* answer calls from employees, usually via 800 numbers. Operators confirm the employee's location, and ask whether he needs assistance.
- *Alternate communications plans* are implemented when all standard organizational communications are lost. These plans may rely on private radio, cellular or satellite phones, and Internet communications, all of which should be monitored during a crisis.

PHASE 10

During phase 10, also known as *the integration phase,* the organization tries to align its business continuity plan with the plans and strategies of its clients, business partners, and regulatory agencies. These parties are integral in the organization's continued success; therefore, their objectives should never conflict, and should support each other whenever possible. Proper alignment may require a complete redo of the business continuity planning process. The business continuity planner should archive all BIA and risk analysis documentation using the highest possible security. This documentation should be reviewed once a year, or whenever the following situations arise: structural changes within the organization; management changes; business process changes; and any changes to the client base.

CHANGE MANAGEMENT

Configuration control manages the configuration of production systems. It ensures that any changes are formally tested and sent through the change management process. *Emergency changes* are made when a system becomes subject to frequent interruption. Although they are implemented more rapidly than standard changes, they still must be approved by senior management before they are put into effect. After the implementation of emergency changes, the changes must be tested and analyzed to determine if they are causing problems. Successful changes may remain permanently, but unsuccessful changes should be removed as soon as possible. Changes should not be implemented unless they receive the proper *change authorization* from management. Once authorization has been given and the change has been implemented, it should never exceed its authorized scope. Change authorization is part of life-cycle management and should not be skipped.

Management Controls

Management controls create and implement policies and procedures that support IT personnel and technical controls. IT service delivery uses the following types of management controls:

- *Software licensing* – Management should legally obtain a software license for every computer operating system, individual application, and utility used by the organization. Auditors should ensure that all licenses are properly controlled and managed; otherwise, the organization may incur harsh legal penalties if it is violating copyright laws.
- *Asset disposal* – When an organization must erase information assets (data), all remnants of that data within the system must be eliminated and destroyed so that recovery is impossible. Auditors should ensure the organization is following proper disposal procedures. The disk should be completely wiped or degaussed; simply reformatting the disk will not eliminate the data. If physical assets must be disposed of, the organization can choose to sell, donate, or destroy them.
- *Asset/media tracking* – All technology, media, and information assets should be tracked, labeled, and controlled with a physical asset program. These controls function on both detective levels (auditing inventory labels) and preventive levels (labeling). Tracking responsibilities fall to the media librarian, who must be able to produce evidence of the existence of this control.
- *User training* – Users must be trained on new software programs, attend seminars, take security training, etc. Trained users can better support IT objectives and identify potential problems.
- *Procedures versus actual work* – Auditors should ensure that procedures are generating the expected work results.
- *Ineffective controls* – Even if controls are ineffective or inefficient, they may possess certain benefits that can be carried over into the next control; therefore, management should review ineffective controls.

System Monitoring

The goal of system monitoring is identifying problems with system operations. IT uses three primary types of system monitoring:

- *Centralized system logging* (or *syslog*) transmits copies of the system log to a specific workstation, where the information is translated into a usable form and reviewed for inconsistencies.
- *Hardware* is monitored and reviewed for errors and workload utilization, both of which forecast future events that may alter system availability. System alert logs and hardware conditions should all be reviewed for workload utilization.
- *Software* includes both event and audit logs, which are captured and reviewed for errors, unsuccessful and successful login activities, and changes to system configuration.

Problem Management

Problem management involves implementing various procedures and methods, such as problem escalation, when certain circumstances arise. These circumstances include the following:

- *Incident handling* is a corrective control. By following certain procedures, the IT response team investigates all reported incidents. The response team should receive training in the types of incidents that constitute criminal activity.
- *Acceptable use policy, or AUP*, violations occur when organizational resources are misused. Human resources should be notified, and the correct incident-handling responses should be implemented.
- *Training* is the process of instructing employees in their job functions, and the handling of problems related to those functions.
- *Job accounting* is the process of ensuring that all requirements of a particular job function are fulfilled, especially those job requirements related to computer programming. Potential problems in job accounting can be recognized through certain indicators, such as jobs that are being completed too quickly or too slowly.

Service, Performance and Capacity

The primary concern of any *IT service delivery audit* is ensuring that data items are being labeled, tracked, managed by properly trained personnel, and delivered efficiently and punctually. When evaluating *IT performance*, auditors will examine three primary performance indicators: IT budget, user satisfaction and technical indicators, especially performance metrics. *Capacity management* monitors system resource usage and estimates the future capacity needs of the system. The tools of capacity management include system utilization reports, which analyze existing resource usage to predict future resource consumption. IT management should also identify *single points of failure*, which exist in every system and usually result from redundancy costs.

Data Processing Centers

Because the data processing center and wiring closets contain a number of valuable organizational assets (computers, wires, network equipment, etc.), they require special physical controls to prevent damage and information loss. The changeover between main power and generator power is handled by the UPS system, which recharges its batteries using the generators. These include a specific set of environmental controls:

- *Emergency power off (EPO) switch* immediately stops the flow of electrical power into the processing center, in order to prevent electrocutions. It should be positioned near the exit door, covered in plastic, and tied into the fire suppression system.
- *Dual power leads* connect to two separate power substations, and help avert power outages. To prevent the expenses associated with running power cables, the data processing center should be built near area power grids.
- *Uninterruptible power supply (UPS)* is capable of monitoring the flow of electrical power to the processing center and activating reserve battery power in the event of a power outage. Before the reserve battery runs out, the UPS will trigger a shutdown within the computers.
- *Standby generators* can power the data processing center during a main power outage. These generators are usually powered by some form of fuel: *Diesel generators* should have a fuel storage capacity of 12 hours, although some organizations may store between 3 and 30 days worth of fuel. *Natural gas generators* are hooked to a utility pipeline, often through a storage tank, negating the need for refilling from a fuel truck. These pipelines offer continuous power over a long time period.
- *Power transfer system* switches from commercial power over to UPS battery power in the event of a main power outage. The switchover is normally programmed to occur automatically; however, because the automatic switch may go offline during a power outage, or may be unable to cope with multiple outages over a short period of time, the organization should have a set of manual transfer procedures.
- *Ventilation and air-conditioning* help maintain the cool temperatures in which computer processing performs most efficiently. The temperature of computer circuitry should not exceed 104 degrees. Temperatures in excess of 115 degrees can cause physical damage.
- *Heating* prevents computer equipment from freezing.
- *Water detection systems* notify IT personnel of any leaks (plumbing, condensation, or otherwise) that may damage computers within the processing center.
- *Fire detection systems* must be installed within the data processing center and other sensitive areas. These systems include the following:
    - *Smoke detectors* use either optical or radioactive smoke detection equipment.
    - *Flame detectors* detect either the radiation or pulsation of a flame.

  - *Heat detectors* go off in the event of a rapid rise in temperature or a temperature reading exceeding 200 degrees.
- The *fire suppression system* responds when one of the above detection systems goes off. Fire suppression involves one of the following systems:
  - *Wet pipe systems* release stored water when a pin is melted, which mechanically opens a valve.
  - *Dry pipe systems* release compressed air prior to releasing water. This has the advantage of activating the EPO switch and cutting off electrical power.
  - *Dry chemical systems* release dry chemicals rather than water. This requires special procedures, because dry chemicals may be poisonous.

Safe Storage and Transport

Safe storage protects against fire, theft, intentional damage, and various forms of environmental wear. Standard business documents and records should be stored in fireproof filing cabinets, and tapes and media disks should be kept in fireproof safes. Organizations rely on two kinds of safe storage: *on-site* and *off-site*. The off-site facility should be a secured building with continuous monitoring. It normally stores backup copies of important documents, files, and electronic storage media. If the organization has contracted a third party vendor to provide off-site storage, the vendor should refrain from advertising storage contents. Regardless of who is providing off-site storage, the organization must ensure *safe media transport*, which involves the proper boxing, labeling, encrypting, and tracking of data before and during shipment. The tape librarian is responsible for tracking media as it is shipped and confirming that it has arrived safely.

Methods for Disposal

In most cases, data assets and storage media are disposed of after they have completed their lifecycles; otherwise, the organization risks exposing sensitive information. The disposal procedure must receive formal authorization and follow a properly controlled process. Organizations dispose of data in a manner determined by its storage medium. For instance*, nondurable media* such as paper documents, photographs, and plastic can be burned or shredded. *Durable media,* such as magnetic tapes and disks, must be disposed of using one of the following methods:

- *Overwriting* involves deleting and overwriting a data file. Simply deleting the information may be insufficient, because deleted files can be recovered. Every single character of data must be overwritten with a random value.
- *Degaussing* exposes the magnetic media to a powerful electromagnet, which erases the data.

Auditor's Concerns

When evaluating business continuity plans, an auditor should do the following:

- Ensure that the business continuity plan is properly secured and controlled. The plan contains vital organization information (such as priorities, blueprints, and trade secrets).
- Determine if archived records have been organized well enough to allow full recovery after a disaster.
- Ensure that both the BIA and risk analysis are supporting management objectives.
- Review the results of the most current business continuity plan test. Testing is important because it identifies and corrects problems.
- Determine whether or not the recovery time objectives (RTOs) are realistic and can be fulfilled by existing equipment.
- Evaluate the organization's procedures for handling work backlogs.
- Ensure the presence of timelines in business continuity documentation. Timelines help disaster recovery by using RTO, RPO, and SDO prioritizations.

Important Terms

Decompiling: The act of dividing a large auditing task into smaller audits so all objectives and requirements can be met.

Modular stage: A type of audit created by decompiling.

Due care: The degree of care for a client that auditors must demonstrate when conducting audits. It is determined by the amount of risk an audit poses. There are three levels of care.

Negligence: Occurs when an auditor fails to demonstrate due care for the client.

Basic care: The minimum level of care an auditor must demonstrate to avoid negligence.

Ordinary care: A moderate level of care.

Extraordinary care: The highest level of care, which most auditors would not be required to demonstrate.

How to Overcome Test Anxiety

Just the thought of taking a test is enough to make most people a little nervous. A test is an important event that can have a long-term impact on your future, so it's important to take it seriously and it's natural to feel anxious about performing well. But just because anxiety is normal, that doesn't mean that it's helpful in test taking, or that you should simply accept it as part of your life. Anxiety can have a variety of effects. These effects can be mild, like making you feel slightly nervous, or severe, like blocking your ability to focus or remember even a simple detail.

If you experience test anxiety—whether severe or mild—it's important to know how to beat it. To discover this, first you need to understand what causes test anxiety.

Causes of Test Anxiety

While we often think of anxiety as an uncontrollable emotional state, it can actually be caused by simple, practical things. One of the most common causes of test anxiety is that a person does not feel adequately prepared for their test. This feeling can be the result of many different issues such as poor study habits or lack of organization, but the most common culprit is time management. Starting to study too late, failing to organize your study time to cover all of the material, or being distracted while you study will mean that you're not well prepared for the test. This may lead to cramming the night before, which will cause you to be physically and mentally exhausted for the test. Poor time management also contributes to feelings of stress, fear, and hopelessness as you realize you are not well prepared but don't know what to do about it.

Other times, test anxiety is not related to your preparation for the test but comes from unresolved fear. This may be a past failure on a test, or poor performance on tests in general. It may come from comparing yourself to others who seem to be performing better or from the stress of living up to expectations. Anxiety may be driven by fears of the future—how failure on this test would affect your educational and career goals. These fears are often completely irrational, but they can still negatively impact your test performance.

Elements of Test Anxiety

As mentioned earlier, test anxiety is considered to be an emotional state, but it has physical and mental components as well. Sometimes you may not even realize that you are suffering from test anxiety until you notice the physical symptoms. These can include trembling hands, rapid heartbeat, sweating, nausea, and tense muscles. Extreme anxiety may lead to fainting or vomiting. Obviously, any of these symptoms can have a negative impact on testing. It is important to recognize them as soon as they begin to occur so that you can address the problem before it damages your performance.

The mental components of test anxiety include trouble focusing and inability to remember learned information. During a test, your mind is on high alert, which can help you recall information and stay focused for an extended period of time. However, anxiety interferes with your mind's natural processes, causing you to blank out, even on the questions you know well. The strain of testing during anxiety makes it difficult to stay focused, especially on a test that may take several hours. Extreme anxiety can take a huge mental toll, making it difficult not only to recall test information but even to understand the test questions or pull your thoughts together.

Effects of Test Anxiety

Test anxiety is like a disease—if left untreated, it will get progressively worse. Anxiety leads to poor performance, and this reinforces the feelings of fear and failure, which in turn lead to poor performances on subsequent tests. It can grow from a mild nervousness to a crippling condition. If allowed to progress, test anxiety can have a big impact on your schooling, and consequently on your future.

Test anxiety can spread to other parts of your life. Anxiety on tests can become anxiety in any stressful situation, and blanking on a test can turn into panicking in a job situation. But fortunately, you don't have to let anxiety rule your testing and determine your grades. There are a number of relatively simple steps you can take to move past anxiety and function normally on a test and in the rest of life.

Physical Steps for Beating Test Anxiety

While test anxiety is a serious problem, the good news is that it can be overcome. It doesn't have to control your ability to think and remember information. While it may take time, you can begin taking steps today to beat anxiety.

Just as your first hint that you may be struggling with anxiety comes from the physical symptoms, the first step to treating it is also physical. Rest is crucial for having a clear, strong mind. If you are tired, it is much easier to give in to anxiety. But if you establish good sleep habits, your body and mind will be ready to perform optimally, without the strain of exhaustion. Additionally, sleeping well helps you to retain information better, so you're more likely to recall the answers when you see the test questions.

Getting good sleep means more than going to bed on time. It's important to allow your brain time to relax. Take study breaks from time to time so it doesn't get overworked, and don't study right before bed. Take time to rest your mind before trying to rest your body, or you may find it difficult to fall asleep.

Along with sleep, other aspects of physical health are important in preparing for a test. Good nutrition is vital for good brain function. Sugary foods and drinks may give a burst of energy but this burst is followed by a crash, both physically and emotionally. Instead, fuel your body with protein and vitamin-rich foods.

Also, drink plenty of water. Dehydration can lead to headaches and exhaustion, especially if your brain is already under stress from the rigors of the test. Particularly if your test is a long one, drink water during the breaks. And if possible, take an energy-boosting snack to eat between sections.

Along with sleep and diet, a third important part of physical health is exercise. Maintaining a steady workout schedule is helpful, but even taking 5-minute study breaks to walk can help get your blood pumping faster and clear your head. Exercise also releases endorphins, which contribute to a positive feeling and can help combat test anxiety.

When you nurture your physical health, you are also contributing to your mental health. If your body is healthy, your mind is much more likely to be healthy as well. So take time to rest, nourish your body with healthy food and water, and get moving as much as possible. Taking these physical steps will make you stronger and more able to take the mental steps necessary to overcome test anxiety.

Mental Steps for Beating Test Anxiety

Working on the mental side of test anxiety can be more challenging, but as with the physical side, there are clear steps you can take to overcome it. As mentioned earlier, test anxiety often stems from lack of preparation, so the obvious solution is to prepare for the test. Effective studying may be the most important weapon you have for beating test anxiety, but you can and should employ several other mental tools to combat fear.

First, boost your confidence by reminding yourself of past success—tests or projects that you aced. If you're putting as much effort into preparing for this test as you did for those, there's no reason you should expect to fail here. Work hard to prepare; then trust your preparation.

Second, surround yourself with encouraging people. It can be helpful to find a study group, but be sure that the people you're around will encourage a positive attitude. If you spend time with others who are anxious or cynical, this will only contribute to your own anxiety. Look for others who are motivated to study hard from a desire to succeed, not from a fear of failure.

Third, reward yourself. A test is physically and mentally tiring, even without anxiety, and it can be helpful to have something to look forward to. Plan an activity following the test, regardless of the outcome, such as going to a movie or getting ice cream.

When you are taking the test, if you find yourself beginning to feel anxious, remind yourself that you know the material. Visualize successfully completing the test. Then take a few deep, relaxing breaths and return to it. Work through the questions carefully but with confidence, knowing that you are capable of succeeding.

Developing a healthy mental approach to test taking will also aid in other areas of life. Test anxiety affects more than just the actual test—it can be damaging to your mental health and even contribute to depression. It's important to beat test anxiety before it becomes a problem for more than testing.

Study Strategy

Being prepared for the test is necessary to combat anxiety, but what does being prepared look like? You may study for hours on end and still not feel prepared. What you need is a strategy for test prep. The next few pages outline our recommended steps to help you plan out and conquer the challenge of preparation.

Step 1: Scope Out the Test

Learn everything you can about the format (multiple choice, essay, etc.) and what will be on the test. Gather any study materials, course outlines, or sample exams that may be available. Not only will this help you to prepare, but knowing what to expect can help to alleviate test anxiety.

Step 2: Map Out the Material

Look through the textbook or study guide and make note of how many chapters or sections it has. Then divide these over the time you have. For example, if a book has 15 chapters and you have five days to study, you need to cover three chapters each day. Even better, if you have the time, leave an extra day at the end for overall review after you have gone through the material in depth.

If time is limited, you may need to prioritize the material. Look through it and make note of which sections you think you already have a good grasp on, and which need review. While you are studying, skim quickly through the familiar sections and take more time on the challenging parts. Write out your plan so you don't get lost as you go. Having a written plan also helps you feel more in control of the study, so anxiety is less likely to arise from feeling overwhelmed at the amount to cover.

Step 3: Gather Your Tools

Decide what study method works best for you. Do you prefer to highlight in the book as you study and then go back over the highlighted portions? Or do you type out notes of the important information? Or is it helpful to make flashcards that you can carry with you? Assemble the pens, index cards, highlighters, post-it notes, and any other materials you may need so you won't be distracted by getting up to find things while you study.

If you're having a hard time retaining the information or organizing your notes, experiment with different methods. For example, try color-coding by subject with colored pens, highlighters, or post-it notes. If you learn better by hearing, try recording yourself reading your notes so you can listen while in the car, working out, or simply sitting at your desk. Ask a friend to quiz you from your flashcards, or try teaching someone the material to solidify it in your mind.

Step 4: Create Your Environment

It's important to avoid distractions while you study. This includes both the obvious distractions like visitors and the subtle distractions like an uncomfortable chair (or a too-comfortable couch that makes you want to fall asleep). Set up the best study environment possible: good lighting and a comfortable work area. If background music helps you focus, you may want to turn it on, but otherwise keep the room quiet. If you are using a computer to take notes, be sure you don't have any other windows open, especially applications like social media, games, or anything else that could distract you. Silence your phone and turn off notifications. Be sure to keep water close by so you stay hydrated while you study (but avoid unhealthy drinks and snacks).

Also, take into account the best time of day to study. Are you freshest first thing in the morning? Try to set aside some time then to work through the material. Is your mind clearer in the afternoon or evening? Schedule your study session then. Another method is to study at the same time of day that you will take the test, so that your brain gets used to working on the material at that time and will be ready to focus at test time.

Step 5: Study!

Once you have done all the study preparation, it's time to settle into the actual studying. Sit down, take a few moments to settle your mind so you can focus, and begin to follow your study plan. Don't give in to distractions or let yourself procrastinate. This is your time to prepare so you'll be ready to fearlessly approach the test. Make the most of the time and stay focused.

Of course, you don't want to burn out. If you study too long you may find that you're not retaining the information very well. Take regular study breaks. For example, taking five minutes out of every hour to walk briskly, breathing deeply and swinging your arms, can help your mind stay fresh.

As you get to the end of each chapter or section, it's a good idea to do a quick review. Remind yourself of what you learned and work on any difficult parts. When you feel that you've mastered the material, move on to the next part. At the end of your study session, briefly skim through your notes again.

But while review is helpful, cramming last minute is NOT. If at all possible, work ahead so that you won't need to fit all your study into the last day. Cramming overloads your brain with more information than it can process and retain, and your tired mind may struggle to recall even previously learned information when it is overwhelmed with last-minute study. Also, the urgent nature of cramming and the stress placed on your brain contribute to anxiety. You'll be more likely to go to the test feeling unprepared and having trouble thinking clearly.

So don't cram, and don't stay up late before the test, even just to review your notes at a leisurely pace. Your brain needs rest more than it needs to go over the information again. In fact, plan to finish your studies by noon or early afternoon the day before the test. Give your brain the rest of the day to relax or focus on other things, and get a good night's sleep. Then you will be fresh for the test and better able to recall what you've studied.

Step 6: Take a Practice Test

Many courses offer sample tests, either online or in the study materials. This is an excellent resource to check whether you have mastered the material, as well as to prepare for the test format and environment.

Check the test format ahead of time: the number of questions, the type (multiple choice, free response, etc.), and the time limit. Then create a plan for working through them. For example, if you have 30 minutes to take a 60-question test, your limit is 30 seconds per question. Spend less time on the questions you know well so that you can take more time on the difficult ones.

If you have time to take several practice tests, take the first one open book, with no time limit. Work through the questions at your own pace and make sure you fully understand them. Gradually work up to taking a test under test conditions: sit at a desk with all study materials put away and set a timer. Pace yourself to make sure you finish the test with time to spare and go back to check your answers if you have time.

After each test, check your answers. On the questions you missed, be sure you understand why you missed them. Did you misread the question (tests can use tricky wording)? Did you forget the information? Or was it something you hadn't learned? Go back and study any shaky areas that the practice tests reveal.

Taking these tests not only helps with your grade, but also aids in combating test anxiety. If you're already used to the test conditions, you're less likely to worry about it, and working through tests until you're scoring well gives you a confidence boost. Go through the practice tests until you feel comfortable, and then you can go into the test knowing that you're ready for it.

Test Tips

On test day, you should be confident, knowing that you've prepared well and are ready to answer the questions. But aside from preparation, there are several test day strategies you can employ to maximize your performance.

First, as stated before, get a good night's sleep the night before the test (and for several nights before that, if possible). Go into the test with a fresh, alert mind rather than staying up late to study.

Try not to change too much about your normal routine on the day of the test. It's important to eat a nutritious breakfast, but if you normally don't eat breakfast at all, consider eating just a protein bar. If you're a coffee drinker, go ahead and have your normal coffee. Just make sure you time it so that the caffeine doesn't wear off right in the middle of your test. Avoid sugary beverages, and drink enough water to stay hydrated but not so much that you need a restroom break 10 minutes into the test. If your test isn't first thing in the morning, consider going for a walk or doing a light workout before the test to get your blood flowing.

Allow yourself enough time to get ready, and leave for the test with plenty of time to spare so you won't have the anxiety of scrambling to arrive in time. Another reason to be early is to select a good seat. It's helpful to sit away from doors and windows, which can be distracting. Find a good seat, get out your supplies, and settle your mind before the test begins.

When the test begins, start by going over the instructions carefully, even if you already know what to expect. Make sure you avoid any careless mistakes by following the directions.

Then begin working through the questions, pacing yourself as you've practiced. If you're not sure on an answer, don't spend too much time on it, and don't let it shake your confidence. Either skip it and come back later, or eliminate as many wrong answers as possible and guess among the remaining ones. Don't dwell on these questions as you continue—put them out of your mind and focus on what lies ahead.

Be sure to read all of the answer choices, even if you're sure the first one is the right answer. Sometimes you'll find a better one if you keep reading. But don't second-guess yourself if you do immediately know the answer. Your gut instinct is usually right. Don't let test anxiety rob you of the information you know.

If you have time at the end of the test (and if the test format allows), go back and review your answers. Be cautious about changing any, since your first instinct tends to be correct, but make sure you didn't misread any of the questions or accidentally mark the wrong answer choice. Look over any you skipped and make an educated guess.

At the end, leave the test feeling confident. You've done your best, so don't waste time worrying about your performance or wishing you could change anything. Instead, celebrate the successful completion of this test. And finally, use this test to learn how to deal with anxiety even better next time.

Review Video: Test Anxiety
Visit mometrix.com/academy and enter code: 100340

Important Qualification

Not all anxiety is created equal. If your test anxiety is causing major issues in your life beyond the classroom or testing center, or if you are experiencing troubling physical symptoms related to your anxiety, it may be a sign of a serious physiological or psychological condition. If this sounds like your situation, we strongly encourage you to seek professional help.

Online Resources

Due to our efforts to try to keep this book to a manageable length, we've created a link that will give you access to all of your online resources:

mometrix.com/resources719/cisa

It's Your Moment, Let's Celebrate It!

Share your story @mometrixtestpreparation